Digging

Susan M. Foster

Digging

Lifting the Memorable
from Within the Unthinkable

Susan M. Rostan

Rosalie Ink Publications • Cold Spring Harbor, New York

For Ella
and
Marian

© 2013 by Susan M. Rostan • www.susanmrostan.com • All Rights Reserved
Rosalie Ink Publications, Cold Spring Harbor, NY • Design, Inger Gibb Graphics
Cover, Lianne Rostan
Printed in the United States of America
Library of Congress Control Number: 2013945845
ISBN: 978-0-9711869-8-9

Acknowledgements

This book exists thanks to the empathy and courage of our uncle, Marian Rosenbloom. Not only did Uncle Marian survive the Warsaw Ghetto and the horrific challenges of the Holocaust, but he dared to venture into the memory of its cruelties each time he unearthed another fragment of his family's buried history.

Friends and family have supported my efforts through their encouragement and reactions to the emerging manuscript. I especially thank Deedee Wigler and Jack Gentile for their honest critiques; my husband Bobby for his encouragement, memories, and insights; our children Seth, Adam, and daughter-in-law Lisa for their supportive comments, and Lianne for her artwork and critical eye; Bobby's sister Yael and cousin Eliane for sharing their memories; my mother Joan Hickok, who spent hours talking about this project and reading pages — encouraging me to write; and especially my granddaughter and muse, Ella.

I am forever grateful to the Drabich family — Aleksandra Komska, Jakub Drabich, and Aleksander Kopiński — for their help documenting the life and death of Stanislaw Drabich.

Above all my editor Terry Walton, for encouraging me to pursue a challenging project and for her dedication, reliability, intelligence, and efficiency.

Timeline – Warsaw and Beyond

Jan 19, 1917   *Elzbieta (Esther Rachel; later Elizabeth) Rozenblum born to Israel and Rivka Rozenblum in Warsaw*

Mar 7, 1930   *Marian and Menache Rozenblum born in Warsaw*

Feb 1938   *Elzbieta marries Benjamin Rutman at age 21*

Sep 1, 1939   Germany invades Poland

Sep 27, 1939   Warsaw surrenders to Germany

Nov 23   Jewish badge made compulsory

Jan 21, 1940   Gestapo orders registration of Jewish property

Sep   Quarantine area set up, later to be called Ghetto, contains 240,000 Jews and 80,000 Christians

Oct 16   Christians ordered to move out of quarantine area and Jews to move in

Nov 16   Warsaw Ghetto sealed off

Jan 1941   378,979 Jews reported in Ghetto

Dec 7   Pearl Harbor leads to withdrawal of American relief organization

Dec 11   Germany declares war on United States

Jul 1942   Verified news of extermination camp at Treblinka

Sep 1-7   *Rivka and Menache Rozenblum selected and deported to Treblinka; Ytel Rozenfarb selected and deported; Marian rescued from selection*

Jan 18, 1943   *Marian leaves Ghetto before first organized armed resistance and second extermination and deportation operations begin; only 40,000 of 380,000 Jews left in Ghetto*

Apr 19-May 16   Warsaw Ghetto Uprising in full force; Germans liquidate Ghetto

Dec 2   *Marian and Elzbieta escape Gestapo*

Mar 1944   *Marian leaves "safety" of Praga, returns to Warsaw proper, hides in apartment house basement*

Aug 1   Polish Uprising begins

Spring 1945   Red Army expels last German troops from Poland in March, several weeks before final Allied victory in Europe; May 8

Dec 1945   *Marian living in Zatrzebie along with Jadzia*

Mar 7, 1949   *Robert Justin Rostan born outside of Paris*

Apr 24, 1956   *Elzbieta and Robert arrive in U.S.*

Jan 12, 2000   *Elzbieta dies*

Apr 3, 2007   *Great-granddaughter Ella is born*

Contents

Elzbieta, most likely from Polish identification papers in 1943.

In memory of Elzbieta Rozenblum
1917-2000

Preface

Where does one begin the story of a family who survived the Holocaust, survived the Warsaw Ghetto, and lived their lives forgetting — trying to forget — what they had endured? Where does Marian Rozenblum's story begin? And how does one find the beginning of his sister Elizabeth's story, when she did not, and then could not, tell us while she was alive? Stories begin when you find the moment in time that signals the beginning of momentum.

• • •

I received a phone call from Elizabeth's stepson one cold winter afternoon many years ago. We hadn't spoken recently but I had no problem expressing my condolences when he told me that his father had died. David — my husband's stepfather — had long been ill and news of his death did not come as a surprise. It had been years since David had arranged for my mother-in-law Elizabeth — lost to dementia at only sixty-nine years old — to live her final years in a nursing home. After Elizabeth left his apartment, David's own failing health and associated difficulties had made social contacts rare. My conversation with David's son was cordial, but in no way was I prepared for the funeral and subsequent emotions brought on by the events of the day.

I remember how my husband Bobby stood shivering at his stepfather's gravesite. The bitter cold seemed an appropriate farewell for the man who had provided a safe and secure home for him, but without the fatherly love he craved. Trying to ignore the cold taking over my own body, I thought about Elizabeth and the story Bobby had told me on our way to the cemetery.

Growing up in Manhattan, Bobby had been an active member of his Boy Scout troop and was eager to be the kind of helpful person he was being trained to be. When the scout troop needed parent volunteers to drive troop members to scouting activities around the city, Bobby had been eager to ask David to participate, just as his friends' fathers did. Bobby raced into the apartment, full of excitement for the camping trip as well as David's participation. David's response was direct and very clear: he offered to pay someone else's dad to make the effort. The ache Bobby felt so often as a child was revisited as he told me the story. I watched him stare straight ahead, as he navigated our car. David had rarely surprised him with a genuine act of parental caring or warmth without Elizabeth's intervention.

Standing at the gravesite I tried to feel the compassion for David that Elizabeth had worked so hard for me, as wife to her beloved son, to grasp. I knew little of the circumstances that had brought Elizabeth and David together as husband and wife; I knew much less of the woman who left her native Poland — a Holocaust survivor — for the safety of France, and, with her only child in tow, began life anew in America. Her story had by decision been hidden from my husband, who knew only that he should not ask about her life before he had come into it.

Leaning against Bobby in the hope of sharing his warmth, I tried to pay attention to the funeral ceremony before me. Moving a little closer to the rabbi, who was leaning over the coffin, something begged my attention. In an instant frozen in time, I grasped what I was witnessing: A weather-sculpted tombstone waited to the left of the space that cemetery workers had carved out of the frozen ground; David was being buried next to his first wife. There was no room for Elizabeth. Her final resting place would not be near her husband's.

I nudged Bobby, who was standing to my left, and quietly conveyed what I had realized was happening. Bobby, who had been drifting in and out of his own memories, moved closer to the gravesite and turned back to me with a look of pain on his face. He nodded with his eyes closed and held his index finger up to his mouth: "Shh." He was willing to sacrifice his own comfort for his mother's sake, for whatever sense of pride might still exist. He made it clear with his glance and a shake of his head that he didn't want me to make a scene.

Afterwards, walking back to the car, Bobby turned to his Uncle Marian and whispered—even as he needed to scream: "What the hell?"

"David's son took care of the arrangements," Marian replied.

Neither Marian nor Bobby was prepared for the surprise at the gravesite. "When the time comes, we'll take care of your mom," he said, grabbing Bobby's arm in an affectionate squeeze. Marian walked past David's family, bowing his head in respect, and turned away to find his car.

"It was a marriage of necessity," Bobby reminded me on the way home, eerily reflecting a bygone scene from my own despondent reverie of Elizabeth:

> Elizabeth looked into the eyes of the man sitting before her. He was a good person, she reassured herself, serious but not romantic in his notions of a life together.
>
> "I have a child to think of," was her reply to his proposal of marriage.
>
> "So do I," his response.
>
> "Your child needs loving parents, just as mine does, but you must know that I have a fondness for you but not the kind of love I have known in my past."
>
> "I understand that, but we can still build a comfortable life together. I will provide for you and your son and ask only that you care for me."
>
> "Of course I care, but is that enough?"
>
> "Yes," he replied and reached into the pocket of his sports jacket for the tiny square box.
>
> Elizabeth looked down at the magnificent diamond ring. It was more than she could ever have imagined wearing. She had pushed aside the

thoughts of a thrilling engagement so long ago that this felt unreal.

"Tak. So it will be," she whispered, and smiled at the lonely man sitting on the other side of the table.

Theirs had thus held the unfulfillable promise of a sense of family. Bobby and I both cried after the funeral, understanding the peace of mind that had come to Elizabeth finally, yet at so steep a price.

I could not have understood how these two scenes, both the real and the imaginary, would someday bring forth anything worth remembering; how this ending and the one to follow — with Elizabeth's passing — would usher in the story the family so needed to hear.

• • •

Years later when Elizabeth died, Marian kept his promise to take care of her final resting place, and his own. It wasn't until Elizabeth's great-granddaughter Ella was born that I would begin my journey into Elizabeth's life and family history, intending to create a family tree for Ella.

Raking through the genealogical records that had recently become accessible online, without the need to travel or translate, I had first assembled my own parents' family trees. Despite the choppy lines of descent in archival databanks, I was able to trace their ancestors back at least three more generations. In addition to the stories my Nana Vivian loved to tell, I had some memories of my own to build on.

I actually remember my maternal great-grandmother, Sophia. I can picture her soft white hair — tinted by the rinse she made from the tea bag she left by the bathroom sink — carefully knotted around the crown of her head. I remember too her tear-bleached blue eyes with love in them for me. She was an artist, a talented fashion designer, who had her own business creating high-fashion hats for women. I wasn't named for her but I pretend that I was; Susan Merrill, my given names, are as close a match to "Sussa Meerel," her Yiddish names, as anyone could imagine. Yet adhering to the Jewish custom of naming a newborn for a deceased family member — creating a living record of a family's ancestry — my parents actually named me after Sophia's husband Israel, whom they called Szrul, and my paternal great-grandmother, Molly. I know very little if anything about Molly, but I do remember stories about my great-grandfather Israel's talent for writing poetry, his stay in Palestine before returning to Bessarabia, today's Moldova and part of Ukraine, to marry Sophia. They are wonderful stories!

My Nana Vivian, Sophia's only surviving child, was an artist — a painter, and my first mentor. Her sisters' lives were cut short by illnesses fatal in the early twentieth century. They had been students, university students each one of them, not yet bringing forth their own branches on the family tree. Her storytelling kept her two older sisters' memories alive for her own children, grandchildren, and great-grand-children. She loved to tell us about our relatives both near and distant, keeping names and anecdotal references fresh in our minds. Nana's precious reminiscences, cradled in the palms of her hands, sifted softly through her fingers as she retold them, time and again, never losing her enthusiasm for their content or emotional effects upon us. Nana's stories placing family members clearly in our minds are the roots of my knowledge. They sparked my interest in constructing the endless branching of family trees.

How well I now know, this was not the case for my husband Bobby. He grew up without grandparents, with no stories of his mother Elizabeth's childhood, with barely the first names of those lost family members about whom little was ever spoken. Bobby's Uncle Marian had survived the Holocaust alongside Elizabeth and would rarely discuss his own childhood. His Uncle Adam had remained in France when first Marian, and later Elizabeth and Bobby, came to America. Adam made it clear to Bobby that he was not to ask Marian about life in Poland before, during, or after the war. For Marian, memory was— had been —an excruciating, chest-cracking experience.

It would be several years after our granddaughter Ella's birth when my sense of responsibility for finding Elizabeth's story, for asking Marian to remember the buried stories of his family, sowed the seeds of a reconstructed family history. What I learned — from readings, online searches, correspondence abroad, old photographs, and treasured conversations with Bobby's Uncle Marian — gave me a vision of Elizabeth's life in Poland. Hers was a brave life efficaciously lived. Perhaps it was also tiny Ella's voice calling *me* "Nana" that encouraged me to create narratives to share with her, my own grandchild. What I had once believed I could never ask of either Elizabeth or Marian for my own edification — or to soothe my husband's sense of incompleteness — I found that I could request of Marian for Ella, Elizabeth's sweet great-granddaughter and namesake. Marian's story is thus told from his own recent recollections, oftentimes painful to unearth.

As I came to learn the facts and consider the anecdotal stories of Elizabeth's life, I found myself visualizing her as she lived, loved, and lost, and began again. It could be said that I came to see the world through Elizabeth's eyes. Her story is told in my own imaginings, its content revealed and guided by Marian.

Elizabeth, seemingly set adrift by her husband David's death and the estranging, if not strange, burial, would become firmly embraced in a family and with friends Marian dared to remember. What I could not imagine was what the remembering would mean for Marian. . . .

"This is the eternal origin of art:
a human being confronts a form that wants to
become a work through him. Not a
figment of his soul but something that appears
to the soul and demands the soul's creative
power. What is required is a deed that a man
does with his whole being . . ."

– Martin Buber

Elzbieta, Marian, and Bobby, 1950.

1

Nourishing a Sprout, Spring 2009

"What a wee little part of a person's life are his acts and his words!
His real life is led in his head, and is known to none but himself. . . .
The mass of him is hidden — it and its volcanic fires
that toss and boil, and never rest, night nor day. These are his life,
and they are not written, and cannot be written. . . .
Biographies are but the clothes and buttons of the man —
the biography of the man himself cannot be written."

– Samuel L. Clemens

I was watching my granddaughter Ella, just two years old, and her companion — a four-month-old black lab called LJ — sitting, as usual, with LJ nestled close by Ella's side. They seemed so content in their own particular kind of digging into the moist vegetation of my back yard. I had been doing some digging of my own, the genealogical kind at this stage of our lives, yet thus far without the obvious satisfaction I could see in Ella's smiling blue eyes and LJ's thumping tail.

In search of the history of my husband Bobby's family — his decimated family tree — I had found myself immersed in the rubble of the Holocaust. Precious little information survived the destruction of their Jewish community in Warsaw. I didn't even have verified names of some family members for searching accessible documents. Worse still, I could not ask for help; the Holocaust years were not discussed by my husband's family.

Resigned to pursuing my handful of clues, I turned to writers and historians for a sense of what the family's life might have been like.

Yet a sense of the general terrain of their times was no substitute for the particulars of their lives. Discouraged by the limitations of the information I possessed, I considered the obvious: the family names, along with their stories, would be lost forever.

The unexpected back yard scene before me was a revelation; it gave me insights into the nature of digging, the patience and focus I needed to continue the painful and painstaking work of reconstructing a family's lost history. I resisted the temptation to run for my camera. Ella's effort was beyond a Kodak moment: it was an experience replete with memories and meanings. I needed words to describe what I was seeing and understanding.

As Ella and L J occupied themselves excavating the soil, a third party, engaged in its own version of digging, drew me away from my own ruminations about excavating the buried lives of Ella's ancestors. Here a determined earthworm was seeking the soft black loamy terrain as it moved forward in its journey along the earth. The little worm, seemingly disturbed by the crowded corner of the yard, burrowed and slowly zigzagged off through the lightly vegetated ground. Engulfing dirt as it tunneled, the worm aerated the soil, bringing nutrients to the surface, and cast a rich fertilizer — vital to the soil's health — back into the earth. L J was nearby, his head just touching Ella's soft pudgy thigh. The puppy's nails dug into soil as he enthusiastically removed dirt from the perimeter of a half-buried rock. Obsessively, L J maintained his focus on the dirt surrounding the rock, digging without concern for the debris flying in all directions.

Tiny Ella meanwhile explored a small log-sheltered hole just vacated by the earthworm. Her curious finger bent in its search for the end of the tubular space. Unsuccessful finding the hole's destination, she began to gently pull tiny plants out of the soil and, after examining their roots, transplant the miniature foliage into new holes she meticulously prepared. Turning next toward the earthworm's travels through and over the soil, Ella placed tiny pieces of leaves in its path and offered a soft but firm directive: "eat." It struck me how nurturing both Ella and the earthworm had been in their diggings. Unlike LJ, who was determined to dig and unearth without concern for the consequences, Ella and her terrestrial friend both created an environment for new growth, for beneficial possibilities.

Ella took a moment to sweep her long golden hair from her face with dirt-covered fingers. Brown streaks appeared across her brow and down around her ear. She sighed when I asked if she wanted to go back into the house for a snack. "Not yet," she whispered, and gave me a look filled with dismay at my ignorance. I looked away from the once clean shorts and t-shirt and found a comforting memory of myself, as a child, digging too. I envied all of them: Ella, LJ, and the little earthworm. I vaguely remembered the joy of it a half century ago, and wished that my current task unearthing roots and buried fragments of lives were not so saddening, so painful.

My own family's tree had been relatively easy to construct in recent years. My great-grandmother Sophia with her long white hair, my great-grandfather Israel's gift for poetry, their daughter Vivian, Nana Vivian to me — all the storytelling of my childhood has helped me place my family clearly and lovingly. But sifting through archived records of Polish Jews and my husband's possible ancestors had left me bereft, all too aware of the absence of records of lives lived, lost in time, and ended. The Holocaust's intentions had erased most of the entries in books of birth, marriage, and death. Their stories had been buried long before I met them — the few remaining family members: all survivors of Hitler's attempt to rid the world of Jews. I resigned myself to scratching around the little mound of information my husband's surviving family could and would recall.

My search had been much like the work of that little earthworm. I did find some names and dates of birth, marriage, and death —

nothing more. Yet absorbing the information and understanding the relationships in time and place gave fertile ground to the beginning shoot, off a fragile sapling, that would become my husband's family tree. The more I learned the more I realized that I was just scratching at the surface relationships among so many lives. I couldn't know the whole story, or even a meaningful part of anyone's life — only the remnants of broken branches: some names and dates of events. Yet I found solace in these names, knowing how richly they color a family's history.

My son Adam and his wife Lisa had chosen to name their first child Ella Jane after my husband's mother, known to us as Elizabeth, and Lisa's grandmother Betty Jane. Ella's naming ceremony took place in the same back yard — under a vine-covered arbor near the site of Ella and LJ's later excavations. Closing my eyes for the moment, I envisioned Rabbi Schwartz officiating at the ceremony. He was the one who had married Adam and Lisa and, years earlier, guided Adam through his Bar Mitzvah.

I remembered how Rabbi Schwartz beamed for Ella as he asked the attention of family and friends, all gathered on the lawn sloping down into a maze of mossy paths meandering through islands of shrubs, flowers, and shade-giving trees. Standing under the arbor, beckoning celebrants to a sun-drenched clearing in the woods, the rabbi transformed the quiet garden into a sacred doorway to our Hebrew community. Presenting Ella Jane with her Hebrew name, Eila Yonit, Ella's parents each offered their loving prayers and memories of the grandmothers they honored.

Unlike Lisa, who had known her grandmother for most of her own life, Adam's memories of his grandmother were gathered until he was eight years old. It had been around that time, the year of his older brother's Bar Mitzvah, that his grandmother began to display the effects of a degenerative brain illness, wandering around the party appearing frightened and confused. "My Grandma Elizabeth," Adam began, as he tried not to remember her near the end of her life — agitated, aphasic, and deeply frustrated by her inability to communicate. Hers had been a tortuous end to a brave and vital life. I had no idea how Adam would describe the grandmother he had known when he himself was still a child.

Now in the words he managed to articulate, despite his tears and the tightness in his throat, we would all hear Adam's heartfelt love for Elizabeth. "My Grandma Elizabeth was a creative, strong and witty woman who dedicated her life to helping others. Children were her passion and she gave her love to them, selflessly and completely." Lisa added her own dedication in memory of her grandmother, whom she had known and loved.

We were all moved not only by Adam and Lisa's words, but also by their obvious emotions as they each reached down inside to touch on their own grandmother's essential being. I was grateful that Adam's chosen memories of his Grandma Elizabeth were built upon the foundation of family lore: the Elizabeth who had survived the Holocaust along with the friends and family members she helped rescue. And, the loving grandmother who, despite the constraints of time, distance, and native Polish language, successfully conveyed her love and affection to her three grandchildren. With limited and richly accented English, Grandma Elizabeth swept through my children's lives for short but meaningful visits from home nearby in Manhattan.

Elizabeth's youngest brother Marian took part in Ella's naming cere-mony, offering prayers for her future with a broad smile and tears of joy. The moment was bittersweet for Marian, whose pale blue eyes glistened from the tears he wiped from his cheeks. Stealing a glance as he spoke, I imagined that along with the joy of new life in the family, he once again felt the pain of loss. It was only a handful of years since he had lost his youngest grandson, only a toddler, in an automobile accident that left his daughter-in-law with devastating damage to her brain. Marian held his pain close to his chest, a pain that must have harkened back to his childhood and life of challenge. The smile Marian managed to bring to his own handsome face brought me back to thoughts of the delight Elizabeth would have felt, knowing that we were honoring her life in this beautiful celebration of new possibilities.

The rabbi's prayer for a life filled with wisdom and acts of kindness wafted through the air we breathed in and I added my own wish that Ella, through her own acts of caring and kindness toward others, would mirror her namesake's intrinsic goodness.

Now a year and a half later I was witnessing Ella sitting not too far away from the same archway, articulating Elizabeth's passion for living and nurturing others in one simple word: "eat."

In April 2003 Helen Schary Motro, the daughter of Ola Schary, one of Elizabeth's close friends, described "Elsa" — as she was known by her close friends and family — in a story published in *Newsweek*. In "Bound Together by an Unspeakable Past," Ms Motro characterized Elsa by her "big laugh" and her delight in children's joyous antics. Ms Motro focused her article on how her mother and her close friends, who were also survivors, never stopped fighting their own interior battles — they simply started over without bitterness. Making their love of life and children the foundation of their new life in America, each was able to cope with difficult times and still enjoy living. This was the Elizabeth I knew. What I did not know was that Elizabeth had been known as Elzbieta before she came to this country, and even that was not her given name — it was the name she chose for herself for safety. I also knew nothing of the experiences "Elzbieta" had braved becoming the extraordinary person I knew — the inspiration for her namesake.

When I married Elzbieta's son Bobby, over forty years ago, I found his family a romantic, cultured contrast to my own family, all of whom had been in this country for several generations. My great-grandparents, all four of them, arrived around the 1900s from the part of Europe held, at various times, by Poland, Russia, and Austria. Unlike my own parents' New York accent, Bobby's mother and uncle spoke with a continental tongue. Their accents — Polish, mixed with French and, in Marian's case, some British phrases — were a delight to my suburban New York ears. I had no idea how hard they had worked to learn and then keep those languages, both their native tongue and speech of survival, or how the scars they so successfully concealed with laughter would affect me in the years to come. As understandings began to form — as I came to learn how both Marian's and Elzbieta's lives had been held together by social skills, intimacy, and laughter — I began to recognize how Elzbieta had welcomed me as her daughter-in-law with these beautiful attributes. I would learn to appreciate George Bernard Shaw's noteworthy insight: "Life does not cease to be funny when people die any more than it ceases to be serious when people laugh."

I can picture Elzbieta — her head high, the golden curls always stylishly coiffed and framing her beautiful broad forehead, angular cheekbones, and huge blue eyes — walking through her Upper East Side neighborhood. Her remarkably straight posture made her look taller than her five foot, seven-inch frame. Her bearing signaled a careful upbringing, and her energetic stride a willful comportment through life. Immersing herself in the resources New York City offers — museums, theater, ballet, and concerts — she was a participant in the city's celebration of culture.

I remember visiting Elzbieta at work in the early days of my marriage. She was a salesperson and resident interior decorator at Cepelia, a Fifth Avenue boutique offering Polish arts and crafts to a select Manhattan clientele. She gave her contagious smile to everyone, establishing a bond even before she greeted you with her "ah-lo," the inflected greeting tinged with her particular mixture of Polish and French.

I remember, even more clearly, her laughter. She brought laughter into a conversational exchange at unexpected moments, marking not merely the humor of dialogue, but also her delight in your mere presence. Elzbieta's laughter flowed from her core; she relished the joy of living, of each moment she shared with you — moments that most people, myself included, might fail to hold dear. In our early years together I was still so unaccustomed to spontaneous laughter that sometimes it made me uncomfortable. I tended, in those days, to miss the importance of relishing the smaller moments, sweeping them under the rug of "getting through life." I never knew where Elzbieta's endless delight came from, but I learned to accept its source as the part of her I could never know — the Elzbieta willfully hidden from sight and comprehension.

I knew Elzbieta for sixteen years before she lost the ability to communicate. My memory of her was filled with both the monumental — my marriage to her son and the help she gave us raising our three children and acquiring our own home, and, perhaps more meaningful, the mundane — the little acts of love and generosity that offered glimpses of her character. It will always be a regret to me that I never had the time to share more of my life with my mother-in-law — perhaps because my own parents' marriage had ended in divorce, and my brother and I felt lost in many disappointments. My own repertoire at that time was safer, more in tune with my grandmother's artistic talent and inhibited, quiet nature.

Much as anyone who knew her, I loved Elzbieta. I only wish I had sought a better understanding of her life when she was alive and able to speak, before the mental confusions of the last decade of her life. Now in my reverie, as I watched Ella and LJ digging in my yard, I thought about the story that I would like gradually, appropriately, to reveal to Ella — a story some of which Elzbieta herself had not been able to share.

Elzbieta was the encouraging parent when I decided to go back to school and continue my education. She was the knowledgeable supporter when I sought to bring my artwork to public venues; she made contacts with gallery owners and encouraged me to accompany her in visits to museums, just the two of us. Yet by 1985 at age sixty-eight, Elzbieta was already showing signs of dementia. I lost the opportunity to have the kind of parent I had craved for most of my life. Now with her namesake Ella in our lives, Elzbieta's story is an especially priceless one.

There was little I could remember of the few hints Elzbieta had offered about her earlier life — the years before, during, and just after the war. And yet, I wanted to give Ella the same gift my own grand-mother Nana had given me: a sense of who I was within the family that had endured hardships to make my life possible. I wanted Ella to hear stories of her great-grandmother Elzbieta and Elzbieta's family — forebears my husband and I knew so little about. I was resigned to the impossibility of knowing their lives with certainty. I relished instead the task of imagining. What did they think or do in key moments of their precious lives. . . .

Manhattan, 1980

Elzbieta walked out of the elevator and entered the lobby of her Upper East Side apartment house in Manhattan. The doorman stepped away from his station to open the large glass doors in from East Seventy-third Street. He smiled at this woman who at age sixty-three still had a beautiful glow. She returned his smile with her own wide beam, signaling her affection and appreciation for his attention and warm daily greetings. It was a beautiful sunny day in the city and promised to stay that way for the rest of the day — a day that would require a trip to the local

*Czech butcher on First Avenue, followed by a subway ride
to Pennsylvania Station, and a fifty-five-minute trip to the
Cold Spring Harbor stop on the Long Island Rail Road.*

*Although her son Bobby would pick her up from the
station, she reminded herself to take only a few things
along; too much weight in her shopping bag would tax her
strength before she even arrived. She entered the tiny
butcher shop and, taking in the tantalizing aromas of fresh
meats and old-world breads, was greeted by Steve, the large
apron-clad man behind the counter. "Mrs Lowenthal, what
can I do for you today?" he said, with a smile across his
wide pink face.*

*"Good morning, how are you?" she replied. Her heavily
accented English and huge smile conveyed her delight in
being acknowledged with such enthusiasm. She needed the
usual: "Some head cheese for my son, Robert, and some
Chruschiki for the children," she replied, happy to be sharing news of the visit she was about to make to Long Island.
"Also, a nice piece of the dark rye bread. It's good with the
head cheese."*

*"And, a bone for the dog?" he asked, anticipating the
other item that she always insisted "had to be fresh"—
a large thighbone. He remembered the beautiful Afghan
hound her son had brought into the shop as a puppy.*

*"Yah, yah," she said, laughing at the predictability of
her order and her delight in providing Sheba with a tantalizing bone. "Of course, a bone!" The image of Sheba, waiting at the door when she arrived for a visit, made her smile.
Sheba always stretched in welcome, her long apricot hair
waving as she playfully extended her long legs with lifted
hindquarters and curled-up tail, as if about to pounce.*

Elzbieta loved the dog and enjoyed how she was welcomed, each time she visited, with anticipatory drools.

"Any steaks this time? I have some beautiful shell steaks. Like last time!" the butcher said, encouraging her to spoil her family once again.

Elzbieta thought about the steaks, willing to bring yet another delicacy along, but unsure how she would manage the weight of the package. She held the palm of her right hand up against the side of her face, hesitating just a moment and, with her huge laugh, said "Tak, tak, yes, yes. Thank you." Steve's family needed to eat too, she thought to herself, as she gave him her usual contagious smile. It was a smile of gratitude for providing her with fresh meats and charcuterie for decades. "The children need it . . . need a special dinner," she responded, referring — in her own mind — to her children as well as Steve's.

She put the purchases, wrapped in butcher paper and string, into her shopping bag, carefully placing the white box of flakey cookies on top. She thought about how Bobby always coughed when he ate the powdered sugar on the Chruschiki and how her grandchildren — Seth, Lianne, and little Adam — loved the sugary taste. She laughed aloud thinking about the powder covering their faces. "Tak," Elzbieta said with a smile, "This is good."

2

Marian's Anguish, Summer 2000

"We'll choose knowledge no matter what, we'll maim ourselves
in the process, we'll stick our hands into the flames for it if necessary.
Curiosity is not our only motive: love or grief or despair
or hatred is what drives us on. We'll spy relentlessly on the dead:
we'll open their letters, we'll read their journals, we'll go through their
trash, hoping for a hint, a final word, an explanation,
from those who have deserted us — who've left us holding the bag,
which is often a good deal emptier than we'd supposed."

– Margaret Atwood

U ncle Marian's "set point" is a huge smile and a soft-spoken manner. That is, unless he is expressing political views or having a conversation about injustices. I see the resemblance to pictures of his father, Israel, in their oval-shaped heads and strong angular jaws. After almost eighty years, Marian's pale blue eyes have narrowed — but they still flicker when he smiles. It is his broad grin that you first notice when he reaches out to hug you in a warm embrace. It is his smile that makes Uncle Marian huge and blinds you to his modest five-foot-seven frame.

One of Elzbieta's two remaining brothers, Marian is our only English-speaking key to unearthing the history of my husband's family. He was the only one who could bring to light the Elzbieta none of us could have known. Yet Marian, who survived both the Warsaw Ghetto Uprising and the Polish Uprising, would not relive his own childhood and unearth the story of Elzbieta along with his own story of survival.

He would not even rake through the images and stories of family and friends lost during the war, to help those of us needing to know. I had witnessed this myself, years before I endeavored to ask about the unspeakable, when my husband's cousin Eliane, Elzbieta's niece, questioned Marian about the family's life in Poland during the war.

Eliane, who is two months older than Bobby, had come from home in Montreal for a short visit to New York. Each time I see her I am amazed at the cousins' resemblance to each other and, by an insistent grouping of genetic material, to our daughter Lianne. Eliane carries an energy that beckons for excitement; it was summertime on Long Island, the wind was up for sailing, and she was keen on taking advantage of the beautiful Long Island weather. She was also eager to see Marian, so Bobby arranged for a Sunday visit and a sail.

With the makings of a Sunday brunch we all set sail from Cold Spring Harbor: Bobby and I, Eliane, and Uncle Marian. The wind carried us quickly north through the harbor and out into the Sound. It was there, in the middle of Long Island Sound, the sloop heeled splendidly to port with Bobby delightedly at the helm, that Eliane, much like our puppy LJ, began her determined digging.

"Marian, I have some questions about what actually happened to my family during the war," she said, as if making an important announcement. Eliane ignored Marian's glare and the tenseness in his jaw that made his discomfort and disdain obvious — to Bobby and me.

With a hint of her French accent, Eliane proceeded with her provocative questions: "Did you know what happened on the day my mother and grandmother were taken away? It was September, 1942." Marian, who had spent years hiding alongside Eliane's family during and after the Nazi occupation of Poland, glowered at her with his response: "Why do I need to remember this, for you? It is better not to think about such painful things." He had managed to smile, as he always does, even when he is sucking back the painful thoughts that have tried to engage him through all the years since the war.

Bobby, who is almost six-foot-four, stood with his feet spread and looked straight ahead at the sails, bracing himself as he held the wheel with both hands. The gusty emotional storm, suddenly and tensely felt by us all, overcame the sunshine and southerly wind that had been gently carrying the sailboat. Bobby had grown up knowing his mother's experiences during the war to be a forbidden topic. Much like other children of survivors — the children described by psychologist Aaron Hass as the "second generation" — Bobby felt the Holocaust as a constant presence even though not discussed. The silence was a gulf — an unknowable part of his heritage — always differentiating him from children whose parents had not experienced the Nazis' killing spree. He lived with the gaping hole the spree had left in his family — with his parents and with Marian. It was a strange empty space, familiar yet enigmatic, that all the love he felt from them could not fill. Marian's emotional response, filled with anger and pain, turned the day cold.

Eliane pushed harder nevertheless. Much as with LJ's insistent scratching at the buried rock, she was determined to find what had been hidden from her. Her father had been unable to speak of their family and life in Poland and her mother had been selective in the stories she told. Eliane's mother enjoyed sharing the good parts, like how they used to go skiing at Zakopane, an exclusive alpine resort at the foot of the Tatra Mountains. With both parents now gone, Marian was her last chance to unearth the memories and preserve images of a family's history.

Most of the Rozenblum family — Marian's two aunts, two uncles, and his paternal grandparents — had immigrated to the United States during the 1920s, but his father Israel did not want to leave the lucrative family business he had built in Warsaw. Israel, an industrious entrepreneur, remained in Warsaw with his wife and their six children. With the invasion of Poland in 1939 Marian's family was forced to split up to survive. Israel and his eldest son Adam sought the safety of the Russian border, while nine-year-old twins Marian and Menache with their mother and siblings — Elzbieta and Leon in their early twenties and Hil in his teens — stayed behind in Warsaw.

Rumors of the plans to isolate the Jewish population of Warsaw in a ghetto began to circulate immediately after the German occupation of Poland in 1939. The Warsaw Ghetto was finally established one year later, in the fall of 1940. It would become the largest of the Jewish ghettos established by Nazi Germany in Poland during World War II. Marian, Menache, Elzbieta, and their mother Rivka entered the Ghetto for what they believed would be a safe haven. Leon and Hil remained outside the Ghetto walls working in a German factory, or so I originally thought.

Marian has always credited Elzbieta's large gray-blue eyes, patrician nose, beautiful smile, and huge intellect for having saved his life and the lives of some of her close friends. Passing for a non-Jew, Elzbieta, with blond hair the color of corn silk, had cultivated important connections both inside and outside of the Warsaw Ghetto. Elzbieta's network of friends and associates provided the aid needed to survive — helping Elzbieta smuggle precious food and medicine into the Ghetto. Elzbieta had saved Bobby's father Joseph Rozenfarb along with Joseph's father Jacob and his sister Danka — Eliane's mother. This was essentially all I knew at the time of our Cold Spring Harbor sail.

Marian — visibly shaken by the seemingly dark images thrust before him by Eliane's questions, her determination to find answers — finally looked into her eyes and spoke: "What do you need to know?" It was clear he had no wish to unearth the entire garden site, but would at last venture a few select pathways. Eliane's response was explicit: "What happened when they arrested my Grandmother Ytel?"

Resigned to at least scraping the safe hard-packed surface of his memory, as the boat tacked across the waves of the Sound, Marian began the story of being one of the seven surviving members of the two Warsaw families then known as the Rozenblums and Rozenfarbs.

Inside the confines of the Ghetto, he told us, the two families were able to secure work in German factories operating within the Ghetto walls. Leon Kriger, the Jewish manager of Schultz's factory and a friend of Eliane's family, had found employment for Elzbieta's friends and family, protecting them from deportation and providing them with food. Marian's mother Rivka worked in an office in Toebbens's factory, where Jews made uniforms and shoes for the German soldiers. Young Marian worked in the office as a messenger boy.

"Toebbens was a businessman," Marian would tell me in the months to come. "He took over the school across the street from the Court House and converted it into his workshop. He made clothing, shoes, and hats. I remember that Toebbens offered only one meal a day to his workers: a bowl of broth with a potato and a piece of brown, butterless bread. The privileged status of the doctors who worked there earned them two bowls of soup. Do you know how they ate?" Marian asked, knowing I had no idea what to answer.

"They ate one bowl of soup and stuck a finger in the other, so no one would try to take it from them," Marian would reveal, pulling a contemptuous smile across his face.

Elzbieta, who had been working as a nurse in a doctor's office before the war, assisting the obstetrician, used her professional skills within the Ghetto walls. She helped create an obstetrics clinic while still working as a nurse at Toebbens's factory. Eliane's family — her mother Danka, grandfather Jacob, and uncle Joseph — all worked in Schultz's factory, making shoes and clothing for the German army. With a sharp glance from the corners of his eyes, Marian added that none of them had been hired for their skills in making shoes or uniforms. Nodding to the importance of employment in Ghetto factories, Marian emphasized that Leon Kriger had effectively saved their lives.

We learned too that after the war Marian had been sponsored to enter the United States by one of his father's two sisters, who along with her brothers had settled in Buffalo, New York. Marian had been in the States for only two years when he was drafted into the army and, with what seems like a crazy twist of fate, was sent in 1952 to serve the U.S. in post-war Germany. It was while stationed in Munich that Marian had walked into the police station and requested information on the where-abouts of Leon Kriger. Marian knew by then that Kriger had settled there after a stay in Paris, and the two did meet.

Leon Kriger had worked in the fur business after the war and accu-mulated some wealth, so Marian was surprised when Leon asked him for a personal favor — some after-shave from the Army PX. Years later, having lost everything by money placed in bad investments and a sabo-taged business, Leon would ask Marian for another favor. Accused by Jews of being a Nazi collaborator, Leon needed written testimony describing his efforts to save Marian's family and family friends from deportation to Treblinka. Apparently some survivors — Jews whom he had not been able to help and was forced to turn away — years and lives later turned against him, calling him a collaborator. Marian, his face flushed in indignation, raised his voice as he asserted to Eliane that he had shouted in Leon's defense.

I don't remember how Eliane responded to Marian's story that day. I do know that it was not specifically what she wanted to know, but she was silent as she listened to Marian recreating some of the safest paths through his memories. She may even have heard the story already, or perhaps she had found letters or documents in her mother's effects, explaining the role Leon Kriger had played in her own family's survival. I do remember how telling his story affected Marian, leaving him ashen and disturbingly pensive, and how Bobby turned on the engine and headed back to home port. Eliane sat very still, almost frozen, and unusually quiet, the color drained from her sunbaked face. Staring straight ahead, into her own emotional turmoil, she did not ask for more.

Composing himself for the summation of his revelations, Marian sat quietly. His abruptly pensive demeanor belied his trauma in retelling the story. It was a façade I would experience often in the months to come, when he would at last lay open the images of his childhood. When he had finally looked into Eliane's eyes that first sailing day, and shared a piece of the crashing images and the pain of recollection, he offered only a distant glimpse of his thoughts. Perhaps it was the information inside or outside the Ghetto that Elzbieta had been privy to, or just a sense of imminent danger, he told Eliane, that prompted her to risk finding safe havens for both families outside the Ghetto. His story ended with a nod to the time he spent with Eliane's family beyond the walls of the Ghetto.

A Polish property owner and a Polish farmer had helped Elzbieta secure hiding places for her loved ones until the end of the war, Marian told us. He was not able then to speak of the brothers and mother taken from him and the years of upheaval. Nor was Elzbieta, in all the years I knew her, willing to recount images of the Ghetto years. Given what I had learned from Marian and read in history books, I could only imagine what Elzbieta had lived through, the images she so desperately needed to hide from us.

Many years after that afternoon on the boat, Eliane would refer to the day with a mix of guilt and sadness. She had pushed Marian to talk and she had no easy way to ask for his forgiveness. That moment would come, but first I had to delve slowly and carefully into the protective layer of the family's history, with Marian's help.

Warsaw Ghetto, 1941

Elzbieta had seen the crammed small apartments during her nursing-school years and knew of the absence of privileges she had grown up enjoying. Losing her business and forced by the Nazis to leave so much behind — her home, her possessions, her freedom — emboldened her, awakened every aggressive cell in her body, and heightened her efficacious nature.

Elzbieta tucked away certain precious papers — the life-saving identification she had secured as a nurse in the Ghetto factory. She chose her pocketbook for its lack of style, its lack of the aesthetic she had been raised with and would carry within her for the rest of her life. Packing her contraband into a sash of fabric she secured around her abdomen, Elzbieta moved her hands across her stomach, checking for the desired effect. She eyed the shape of her now protruding belly in the cracked glass of a window in the little alcove where she met her contact. She was satisfied this morning, satisfied that she had created a successful strategy, once again, the telltale form of a pregnant woman.

The food — pieces of meat, some salt and sugar, tied into little satchels, and bread — had become more precious than ever. The medical supplies, once-sterile bandages and analgesics, along with the food, were safely hidden under her loose blouse, tied low to emphasize her blossoming belly. Friends on the Aryan side had enabled her to sneak food into the Ghetto — food for family and friends — and supplies for the obstetrics clinic she managed to create.

Gaining access to the area around the Court House on Leszno Street, where she was making her Ghetto contact today, sent her heart into palpitations. The guards would usually allow anyone through who could state a good reason for being there and her dear friend, a non-Jew and former classmate living outside the Ghetto, had been able to slip her a tightly packed package as they each waited in line to enter, pretending not to know each other. Today, however, someone stopped her and asked her why she was there. She explained that she had business in the Court House and, showing him the special pass, he let her go, but not without asking her for her name. "My name? Elzbieta Rutman," she answered in her perfect Polish and smiled her heartwarming smile. Back then, in 1941, her huge blue eyes sparkled out of necessity.

Elzbieta, wearing the Star of David armband as she walked through the streets leading to the court, placed her life on the line each time she smuggled in a treasured package; knowing it was a necessary risk made it bearable, almost satisfying. She pressed her hand against her abdomen, appearing to experience some pressure from a fetus, but actually searching for telltale signs of the medical supplies she carried. Her nursing training was pushed to its limits as she sought to create safe and sanitary conditions for the women bringing new life into a world committed to their extermination.

Elzbieta, head held high in her beautiful easy stride, worked her way through the dirty streets of the Ghetto —

the abhorrent wastes spilling out into the crowded streets,
the slow stinking death of sick and starving children.
Smelling the ubiquitous odor, she allowed herself to think
only of life.

3

In Marian's Confidence, Summer 2009

"Our sense of worth, of well-being, even our sanity
depends upon our remembering. But, alas, our sense of worth,
our well-being, our sanity also depend upon our forgetting."

– Joyce Appleby

The phone rang and as I lifted the receiver I checked the phone's digital display identifying the caller as Marian. "Hi," I said, in a cheerful welcome, hoping to beat Marian to an introduction. "Sue? It's Marian," he responded, seemingly playing out the script he had prepared as he dialed the phone.

"How are you? How is everyone?" I replied, hoping to hear only good news.

"We're all fine. Listen, Sue, we would like to stop by this weekend, if it's OK with you and Bobby."

"I know we're free on Sunday, how about brunch?" I suggested.

"Sunday is good for us. I'll be coming with the boys, if that's OK with you." "The boys" were Marian's sons Marc and Ira. Marian's wife Carol had difficulty sitting in the car for long trips, making her visits infrequent.

"Great," I answered, trying to ease the discomfort I heard in Marian's short, fact-filled sentences. He was always afraid of imposing but of course we would welcome his sons. The fact that he was living four hours north of my home on Long Island made "downstate" visits rare. I planned the menu before the receiver hit its cradle. We would have the usual: bagels, lox, and cream cheese. I made a mental note to remember bialys, fresh fruit, and a sugarless pie for Marian's restricted diet.

Thus one sun-drenched afternoon — years after the Cold Spring Harbor sail with Eliane and just months after Ella's digging focused my genealogical research — Bobby and I sat on our patio having brunch with Marian. In anticipation of the visit I envisioned segueing our conversation yet again into the past, if only for the names of relatives long gone. Little did I know how far Marian had come in his willingness to talk, at last.

Turning to Marian and his forty-something sons — Marc and Ira (named for Marian's twin Menache and father Israel) — I remember enthusiastically describing how I was trying to create a family tree. The sons would find exploring their ancestry an interesting enterprise, I believed.

As I read my list of the approximate names of Marian's family, noting where I had blanks alongside relationships, Marian seemed more distracted than usual. I noticed Marc and Ira giving each other secret signs and Bobby closing his eyes, probably fearing I had initiated a painful family exchange. Hoping to engage Marian and assure the others that I needed only names, not painful stories, I mentioned my discovery that my mother-in-law's name was actually Estera Rachel, and not Elzbieta, or Elsa, as Marian called her. Marian, whose eyes lifted to meet mine, smiled. "That's correct," he acknowledged in his soft deep voice. "Elzbieta was not a Jewish name. Elsa took that name; she didn't use her given name."

Marian, sitting at the head of the table and dressed, as usual, in a pressed shirt, khakis, and sports jacket, could provide only a few of the names I needed. He could not remember his grandmother's first name, although he did remember her last name — she was "Grandma Wilde." He was limited by what he remembered and what, as a child, he had actually known. Nonetheless, through this simple task Marian began the difficult job of selecting memories to share. As he began speaking of his family I envisioned him transporting the delicate roots of his family's tree to a time and place that was safe for all of us to witness.

With a huge grin on his face and the excitement of the child he had once been, not yet ten years old, Marian began his story, using his characteristic "'kay?" for okay?, an interjection he typically uses to emphasize his point of view. Bobby and I were astounded at the new openness in Marian's words. His sons' eyes opened wide.

"I remember it was 1939, 'kay? My father had just ordered a new Studebaker truck when the Germans invaded Warsaw. The old truck he was using to transport gravel was constantly breaking down, 'kay?, and my father finally decided to buy a new one. Can you imagine the timing? My father lost his deposit!" Marian bellowed, with a laugh that did not hide the frustration he had witnessed so many years and lives ago.

"I thought your father had a lumberyard," Bobby interjected, questioning his own memory as much as Marian's.

"Yes, that's correct," Marian said, glancing at Bobby with a smile that revealed his pride in his father's accomplishments. "My father first had a lumberyard and then, when it was successful, he began manufacturing children's clothes. Your Grandfather Israel," Marian paused, looking at Bobby and then at Marc and Ira, to stress their relationship to the man he was bringing to his mind and, I imagined, to his heart. "Your Grandfather Israel was a successful businessman. The gravel business was just a sideline."

Marian's voice conveyed his pleasure in telling of his father's accomplishments. In his bravado, I heard the young child taking over Marian's adult heart and mind — with a voice submerged so long ago in the service of survival, of being a "mensch."

"Adam and my brother Leon worked for him as salesmen, 'kay?, and he was grooming Leon to take over the family business," Marian added. There was a distinct somberness in his voice now, at the mention of his brothers. I noticed the change in his face, which no longer held a smile.

I mentioned my surprise that his father had been involved in so many differing businesses. "Yes, he was very good at coming up with ideas for businesses and he had enough money to speculate. As a matter of fact, 'kay?, he had just invested in a children's clothing store for Adam before the war." Marian's delight in this additional information returned a sparkle to his eyes.

Gazing straight ahead at no one in particular, Marian sat for a moment, making room for this rush of earlier memories with an obviously pleasant effect — for the happiness and pride he had felt as a young child in Warsaw, well before the war. I was glad to see Marian enjoy his recollections, as he stepped back before the encapsulated horrible experiences and sought safe ground, happy terrain.

I took this moment to gather my thoughts and grab another napkin for notes. I had exhausted the space on the sheet of paper prepared for Marian's visit — the sheet with empty spaces for his grandparents' names, and question marks next to his brothers' English names, as I tentatively identified them. While Marian had been sharing his good pre-war memories, I had been making notes all over my little sheet of paper and then on a handy napkin, lest we lose this welcome momentum.

Nonchalantly, I took a bite of my bagel and tried envisioning the family with Marian's latest information. I could "see" Marian's father Israel, who I knew bore a striking resemblance to Marian. Unlike Marian, who had worked for the same company for decades before retiring, Israel had been a man in constant entrepreneurial motion. Bobby must have been sharing my need to strengthen his own image of Israel, who died when Bobby was only three. I sensed his discomfort, then heard him clear his throat and begin to question Marian about his family.

"Was my grandfather a religious man?" Bobby asked. Knowing how competently Marian performs holiday rituals and his fluent reading of Hebrew texts, Bobby was wondering at the small place religious observance occupies in Marian's daily activities. Had his family's attitudes been changed by their wartime experiences?

"He was religious, but not totally observant," Marian answered. "Like my mother he was an assimilated Jew. Unlike my mother, who wouldn't even write on Saturdays, 'kay?, my father would take the boys to synagogue on Saturdays and then go to work." Marian gave this amusing side of his father with a little chuckle.

"Did you go to public school?" I asked, curious whether Marian's mother had wanted her children to assimilate as well. I realized I had little information about Rivka, not even an image from a worn-out photograph. For us Marian's mother was an abstraction, a presence in Marian's life, but we had no sense of who she was.

"We went to public school, 'kay?, but my mother hired a tutor to come to the house and teach us Hebrew," Marian answered. His now serious expression suggested he would not pursue this part of his life; he was not ready to talk about the brothers he had lost. I would learn in the months to come that Hil, about five years older than Marian, had been an excellent student — studying classical Hebrew and speaking Yiddish as well as Polish. Hil was the only one in the family to gain entrance into the Tarbut high school, a select gymnasium. Part of a Zionist network of Hebrew-language schools offering a secular curriculum, the Tarbut high school educated many of Poland's gifted Jewish students. Rivka had hired the tutor to give her children every possible educational advantage.

Marian hesitated for a long moment, shifting in his chair and wiping beads of sweat that had accumulated on his chin. "Elsa was a nurse before the war," he proudly reminded all of us, using his name for Elzbieta. "But she was also entrepreneurial like our father."

"She had a dental supply business, 'kay?" he added with pride in his voice. "It was just off of Jerusalem Avenue," he stated, revealing, for the first time I had heard, an actual location in what was, before the war, the beautiful prosperous city of Warsaw.

"It was called 'Dentorex,' 'kay? — The King of Dental Supplies,'" he added, spreading his arms as if reading a huge sign in front of him. With Marian's sudden enthusiasm for this continuing story, I was surprised and saddened that this was the first time we had heard him speak of his childhood in this way. Marc and Ira sat quietly, taking in this family history with amazement.

"Elsa owned the dental supply company with her friend Benjamin," he stated matter-of-factly.

I innocently looked up and corrected him: "You mean her first husband, Benjamin." My search for Polish documents connected to Elzbieta had yielded her marriage certificate, along with her given name.

In what seemed like an endless nonplussed pause, Marian again shifted his weight, took a deeper breath, and with his eyes focused on the patio table in front of him, acknowledged his error. "That's correct," he almost whispered. I looked up at Bobby, Elzbieta's only child, the child of her second marriage, and saw his eyes close, bringing himself to a place of safety. Marc and Ira sat motionless, expressionless. It occurred to me that Marian didn't realize Bobby and I knew about Benjamin, who was most likely the love of Elzbieta's life, and that I might have brought too much information to light. The discomfort I felt at this moment — the awkwardness in revealing Marian's attempt to protect Elzbieta's memory — served a greater good. Marian, it seemed, was coming to terms with which parts of Elzbieta's life he could and could not share.

It was at that juncture that I realized how Marian had been creating the context for Elzbieta's story. I don't believe that was his intention, but it was what emerged from the little pieces of stories we heard that afternoon. I would learn about the Elzbieta I had not known but in so doing I would get to know Marian in ways I had not thought possible. In gaining his trust and encouraging him to share stories of his and

Elzbieta's life, we together lessened the emotional distance between himself and our little family.

Marian ended his recollections of Elzbieta's business, and our conversation that day, in describing the days and months after the Nazi occupation of Warsaw. With obvious sadness in his eyes, slow and deliberate speech, and a decidedly lower voice, he told us of the day the Germans, moving into his beloved Warsaw, had confiscated the dental supplies from Dentorex.

"Can you imagine it, 'kay? It took five hours for the Germans to empty the apartment. They took anything they could carry into their trucks. We had no choice but to sit and watch."

Overwhelmed by memory of the raw helplessness blanketing their world, Marian held his head in his hands, took a breath, and released his hands into the air, as if this gesture could facilitate comprehension.

Marian had exhausted his ability to retrieve stories without pain. His calm engaged demeanor made it obvious to all of us, however, that this encounter had been cathartic. Marian had shared what he could and I was anxious to piece it all together. Our two families parted fondly, with no plans for future conversations.

Later Bobby and I sat for a long while, reflecting on Marian's story and, in particular, his initial misrepresentation of Elzbieta's relationship with Benjamin Rutman. Although through Bobby's mother we had known of her marriage to Benjamin, this was the first we had heard of both Elzbieta and Israel being in business with Benjamin. The truck that Israel ordered just before the war was going to replace the worn-out vehicle he and Benjamin had used to start their shared business venture. Apparently, Benjamin had been an integral part of the Rozenblums' lives even before the Germans invaded Warsaw in 1939.

Bobby and I had known about Benjamin for decades but had just two stories to connect to his name. The first took place early in our own marriage, when Elzbieta surprised both of us with the revelations about Benjamin as we drove along the New York Thruway.

Elzbieta loved the mountains of upstate New York and she usually rented a small home on the mountain each summer. We were returning from a weekend together in Hunter, New York, and the drive down the Thruway was unusually long. I remember noticing that Elzbieta, sitting in the back seat tending to our first child, Seth, seemed quieter than usual. I dismissed it as the fatigue to which we had all succumbed. Quite unexpectedly, however, Elzbieta leaned close to our front seats and began a story that my husband had never heard before: she had been married to Benjamin before she married Bobby's father, Joseph. Benjamin was her first love and for some reason she now needed to share this treasured fact with her son and daughter-in-law. I remember wanting to reach for Bobby's hands, which were firmly clutching the steering wheel, hoping to relax and comfort him and keep him focused on the road. I looked down at my hands as they moved toward Bobby's, and pulled them back. My own hands were shaking as Elzbieta continued her story.

Through his own network of friends, Elzbieta's third husband David, Bobby's stepfather, had found Benjamin in South America, where Benjamin had gone after the war. Elzbieta didn't offer us any additional information — what had happened to him during the war, and why hadn't they reconnected? — and we were too stunned to ask. She simply mentioned that knowing he was still alive had been comfort enough for her.

The second story was about the day Benjamin came to see Bobby. He had been in touch with Elzbieta and had begged her to see him and let him meet her only child. They made arrangements and Elzbieta met Benjamin in Manhattan, one afternoon so many years ago. Benjamin stood by at some distance and watched her little boy playing with his friends. Bobby never met him.

Bobby told me that he remembered the incident but of course he had not understood its significance. Learning of the part Benjamin must have played in Elzbieta's early life before the war, the decision to move on with her life without him was hard to fathom. Neither Bobby nor I could possibly know what motivated Elzbieta to end her ties with Benjamin. We could only imagine the depth of her sadness.

Bobby and I had a lot to think about as we continued the excruciatingly unsettling trip home with Elzbieta, still out of sight in the back seat of the car with Seth. Bobby was feeling an old wound for the first time. I could only imagine what was going through his mind as we neared Manhattan. Elzbieta's personal life, as Bobby had known it, had always revolved around him, his surviving uncles, Adam and Marian, and their families and friends. I had met many of Elzbieta's friends during the early years of our marriage. Most were survivors — some were friends from Warsaw and others were friends-of-friends in the network of survivors living in Manhattan. Bobby must now have been wondering about how many of them knew about Benjamin. They all knew so much more than he did about his own mother. His godmother Irene, Elzbieta's closest friend — someone she knew before the war came to Warsaw — must have known Benjamin, known what he had meant to Elzbieta.

Marian would eventually confide to me that four years after the war ended Elzbieta made a painstaking decision to marry Bobby's father, Joseph Rozenfarb. Apparently, through her surviving network of friends and family, she did hear that Benjamin had survived confinement in Siberia. Elzbieta chose not to find him or to return to his side, but Marian would not tell us why. Bobby never knew of the man who would have been his father if the world hadn't fallen apart. Now, as I think about the car ride back from Hunter on the Thruway, I suspect it was Elzbieta's recent knowledge of Benjamin's death that brought the story to her tongue.

Stories about life in Poland had been scarce throughout my husband's childhood. He learned early that his mother withdrew when he

asked questions about their family and life before or during the war —
the topic was never part of their storytelling. Much like Marian's recent
unexpected revelations, during our Sunday brunch on the patio, that
day on the Thruway was amazing. Even I knew that much, back then.

Warsaw, circa 1937

*Elzbieta could not keep her mind off his handsome
face. Standing about five-foot ten, she guessed, he had a
strong body and softly angled eyes. Irene, one of the physi-
cians in the doctors' office, sat smiling as the young nurse
described her beau. Irene could see in Elzbieta's eyes that
this was going to be a serious relationship; Elzbieta was
in love.*

*"What did you do last night?" Irene asked, hoping to
experience just a little bit of Elzbieta's excitement.*

*"We had dinner and took a long walk. He is such a
good listener, always making a good analysis of a problem
I discuss with him. He has a good mind for business."*

*"What kind of business were you discussing?" Irene
asked, wondering what Elzbieta was thinking about besides
her nursing practice. She was an excellent midwife and
Irene didn't want her to lose focus after all her training.
She knew that Elzbieta's brothers, Adam and Leon, were
involved in the family business and worried that Elzbieta's
father Israel might encourage Elzbieta to join them. Israel
had been successful in each of his business ventures and*

now that he was planning to spin off a children's clothing store for Adam, since now he had a wife to support, Irene was worried that Israel would try to encourage Elzbieta to try her own hand at some venture.

"Papa thinks he can make some money transporting gravel," Elzbieta began, "but I'm not sure that it is worth the investment in a commercial truck. He talks about how he can make it work and how he can start with a reconditioned truck, nothing too expensive. I am afraid that he is getting distracted from his manufacturing business. He is doing well and I don't think he should be branching out into something he doesn't know anything about. He says it's just taking gravel from here to there and he can do it faster than the usual horse-drawn carts, which means he can make so many more trips in a day."

"And what does Benjamin think about the plan?" Irene asked, hoping to get a better sense of Benjamin's thinking.

"He thinks it's a great idea! He wants to discuss it with Papa."

"How do you feel about that? Would you want him to go into business with your father?" Irene questioned her dear friend, the woman she had come to love and trust in such a short period of time.

"Well, if Benjamin had a good job, a steady income, we could . . ."

"You could what?" Irene asked, with a little teasing push.

"Papa would say yes if Benjamin asked him for my hand."

"So that's what this is all about," Irene shot back with a chuckle. "The girl's in love and she's trying to make it work

. . . make a marriage." Irene smiled her broad natural grin, the smile that always made Elzbieta feel like a little sister, delighting the woman she adored.

Elzbieta blushed as she smiled back. Growing up with two older brothers left her eager for close girlfriends. In Irene's smile, she saw herself as someone to be loved, to be taken seriously, someone you could trust, and Elzbieta loved her back. She couldn't know, in that moment, that they would grow old together in a life far removed from this one.

4

Inside and Outside the Ghetto, 1939-43

"In such an age I dwelt on earth
when men had fallen so beneath their nature
that they, unbidden, for their lust would kill,
and foaming stagger in the tangles of confusion,
possessed by tainted creeds, bewildered by delusion."

– Miklos Radnoti

Several months after his visit with us out on Long Island, I gave Marian a draft of the story I had written about Elzbieta and the family. He promised to tell me any misunderstandings or mistakes in the information I had gathered. He seemed eager to help, but I did not hear from him for over a month. Then he called one afternoon and asked if he could pay me a visit the following day. We arranged a time when we could be alone. I expected a paper draft covered in red ink. Quite unexpectedly, however, Marian gave me a verbal sketch of his own story, and allowed himself to succumb to the painful recounting of his family's losses. It was as if the first stories encouraged the next, and the next.

Marian startled me with his first response to my preliminary story: "I did not see the Germans kill my brother, Menache, 'kay? I was not there," he said, almost choking on his own words. This was a stunning revelation.

Bobby and I had always believed that Marian had witnessed his twin brother's execution — it was part of unquestioned family lore. We had been wrong and Marian wanted me to know this — that he had been spared at least this much of the trauma of his brother's death. I sat back in my chair and nodded, letting him know that I grasped the enormity of the error and would remove it from my narrative. I couldn't control the rush of blood to my face and the tightening of my gut — I had misrepresented a terrible experience in Marian's life, making it unimaginably more dreadful than it had actually been. I felt over-whelmed by a responsibility to "get it right." Marian, satisfied that I was eager to continue, that I would be conscientious and trustworthy, pro-ceeded with *his* story. That is, as much as he was able to share that day.

"My father, brother Adam, and Benjamin escaped to Russia as soon as the Germans entered Poland. They knew they would have been the first to be arrested, 'kay? Businessmen were on the infamous list of tar-geted Jews. They headed for eastern Poland, occupied by the Russians, knowing they could survive there, they could find some way to earn money to live. We heard they were even doing business when they first arrived. Can you imagine that? But the Russians eventually imprisoned them. They were sent to Siberia along with the other misfortunates." I understood Marian to mean those individuals deemed unfavorable to the Russian regime.

"Some time later we heard that Benjamin, who had married Elsa several years before, 'kay?, had been killed." Marian was trying to be clear about the sequence of events without giving too much detail. I wondered how much he was leaving out and how much was unknow-able to him at the time. I kept reminding myself that his words were the perspective of a child as perceived distantly by an adult.

Soon after the occupation of Warsaw in October 1939, my researches would reveal, a series of special decrees were initiated against the 360,000 Jews living in the city. The intent was apparent — an economic and social ruination of the Jews. Much like the other Jews in Warsaw, Marian's father had to register his property, his bank accounts were frozen, and his factories and businesses expropriated. It was almost impossible for any Jew to earn a living. The Nazis termed the Jewish quarter of Warsaw a quarantine area, directing residents to separate themselves from the dangers of "Typhus-infested Jews." Refugees from the provinces entering Warsaw — both Jewish and Christian, voluntarily or deported — were given no choice but to live in the quarantine area. The Jews of Warsaw were further differentiated by having to wear a special armband — a white band of fabric, ten centimeters wide, with a Star of David.

The Germans had projected the establishment of a ghetto as early as 1939, yet it took a full year for them to create the Warsaw Ghetto. The Jewish Council, or *Judenrat*, headed by Jewish resident Adam Czerniakow, had delayed its establishment arguing that Jews were a valuable labor resource.

Meanwhile, the inhabitants of the "Jewish quarter of Warsaw" were at the mercy of the Nazi soldiers and collaborators whose brutality intensified in the belief that they had a subhuman species at their mercy. The scarcity of food, and the constant threat of being forced into labor brigades with meager rations, made existence untenable for the poorer residents of the district. With news of the first ghetto established in the industrial city of Lodz, the Jews of Warsaw saw their own fate sealed. A decree on October 16, 1940, gave Christians two weeks to move out of the quarantine area and those Jews who remained outside the area to move in. One month later, on November 16, the Warsaw Ghetto was sealed off and within a year, an edict made leaving the Ghetto without permission punishable by death. On December 11, 1941, Germany declared war on the United States, four days after the Japanese bombing of Pearl Harbor.

I remember having a conversation with Marian after the 9/11 Towers left New Yorkers traumatized by fear — the omnipresent fighter jets roaring over my home, patrolling the New York skies, and soldiers, so many soldiers with guns, guarding bridges, transportation centers, and my daughter's Tribeca neighborhood. Feeling the differences between the two situations six decades apart, I asked Marian how long it had taken for him to adjust to a world turned upside down. Marian thought for what felt like mere seconds and responded: "Three weeks." I was more shocked by the short time it took for the Jews to settle into their new world order, than comforted by the hope that in the fall of 2001 we would soon settle into the "scheme of things."

Within the confines of the Ghetto, the Jews of Warsaw slowly began to give and attend lectures, concerts, and courses. Feeling safe behind the Ghetto walls they established community kitchens and institutions for the aged, homeless children, and refugees. It was common knowledge that some Jews worked as informers for the Gestapo, but it was explained as their way of making a living — a despicable livelihood; the Gestapo sought details of merchandise hidden in the Ghetto as well as gold, smuggled food, and medicine. The Jewish Council, a Nazi-sanctioned government-in-miniature, furnished work battalions, maintained peace and order (by Jewish policemen), trained skilled workers, managed sanitation and medical needs, and organized workshops where raw materials allotted by the Germans were finished by Ghetto workers for the armed forces of Germany, the *Wehrmacht*.

"Elzbieta secured an acceptable place for us to stay in the Jewish Residential District," Marian said. He, Menache, and their mother Rivka shared a two-bedroom apartment. Elzbieta had her own apartment where she operated her dental supply business until all the merchandise she managed to salvage had been sold. These were the first of many "accommodations" — including a later stay at a church on Leszno Street, which they would inhabit as the Nazis transformed the Ghetto from a Jewish community to a holding place before eventual deportation to the Treblinka death camp. Elzbieta took charge of the family in the Ghetto, securing their safety and saving their lives, as long as she could. Marian suggested to me, with little detail, the desperation they felt as they began to understand the ramifications of forced expulsion from their home.

By now, Marian's life must have been increasingly restricted, but he did not speak of his experiences in the Ghetto — the lack of food, the intolerable lack of hygiene, and the constant threats to his safety and security. He did not tell me the untellable — the images of starving men, women, and children in the streets of the old town, morphing into corpses lying on the sidewalks, neglected and ignored.

My husband and I would see these images for ourselves in the Fall of 2010, in the Israeli director Yael Hersonski's *A Film Unfinished.* Hersonski juxtaposed raw footage of a Nazi propaganda film of life in the Warsaw Ghetto in 1942, just before the mass deportations to Treblinka, with clips of the Nazis making the film and the reactions of survivors, now well into their eighties, sitting and watching the raw footage. Scenes of people busily walking down a street in the Ghetto, adjusting their paths to avoid a starving child begging for food — their sunken faces devoid of expression, of engagement in life. Or worse still, the throngs of people walking along the sidewalk, stepping around a corpse, as if it were a puddle of mud or dog feces. We would eventually see such images, but not that day with Marian.

I did know then, however, that Emanuel Ringelblum, the Jewish historian who left the world his first-hand documentation of daily events in the Ghetto, up until his death in 1943, penned descriptions of events there and noted the "marked, remarkable indifference to death, which no longer impresses." In August 1941, when Ringelblum made this entry, he also noted that it was rare for anyone to visit relatives in the hospital and there was little interest in the dead — people were capable of walking past corpses with indifference.

Marian was understandably evasive in dealing with the Ghetto years; he noted, quite simply, that the Gestapo found his mother Rivka working in Toebbens's factory in the Ghetto. She had brought Menache to work with her that day in September of 1942, and the Gestapo arrested them both. Earlier, through archived documents from Israel, I had found reference to Rivka perishing in a concentration camp. My husband had known little more than that about his own grandmother.

Marian explained the importance of gold during the war. Gold — even dental gold to be used for fillings that Elzbieta had been able to squirrel away — had made all the difference in the world. Gold was necessary for survival during the war, in and out of the Ghetto. Oftentimes a life-saving commodity, this time it wasn't sufficient; the pieces of gold that each family member had secured into clothing had not saved Rivka's life. Luck, as well as intelligence, played a significant part in a world gone mad. This is all Marian would tell me about his family on this noteworthy first day we sat together — Marian talking and me listening — huddled together at my kitchen table.

I would learn that because it was dangerous to defy German decrees, most assimilated Jews and even converts did not stay outside the Ghetto. They preferred the ostensible safety inside the confines of the Ghetto walls. Some highly acculturated Jews were nevertheless motivated to live on the Aryan side; they felt capable of surviving "on the surface" by passing as non-Jews. Some "principled" Jews, however, made the serious error of having a hostile attitude toward acquiring Aryan papers; until the big deportations in 1942, this was regarded as a kind of desertion.

With Marian it would take some months, and several conversations, before I learned that his brothers Leon and Hil had also entered the Ghetto in 1940, along with Marian, Menache, Elzbieta, and Rivka. As we sat across from each other at my kitchen table in the spring of 2011, Marian would matter-of-factly insert this detail into our conversation. I had been reading aloud the rough draft of a letter he would later submit to Yad Vashem, the Holocaust memorial in Israel. The letter was testimony describing his wartime experiences and the events warranting recognition of a Polish rescuer as one of the Righteous

Among the Nations — the title bestowed upon non-Jewish rescuers during the Holocaust. Marian stopped me and added Leon and Hil's names to the list of Rozenblums living in the Ghetto in 1940.

"Leon worked as a mailman, delivering mail throughout the Ghetto," Marian would tell me. "He was about nineteen."

"And Hil? Did he work in the Ghetto?"

"No, not in the Ghetto. Hil spent most of his time in school or studying," he responded. Hil was fifteen in 1940, and Marian still only ten.

"Did you go to school in the Ghetto?" I asked, referring to the religious schools that had operated, in spite of the German decrees forbidding any schooling.

"I had a tutor. Elsa arranged for a tutor. There were five or six students, at least two girls and three boys that I can remember. It was a secular schooling, 'kay? We all had a secular education. Even Hil, fluent in Hebrew. He wanted to become a dentist," Marian added. "I remember Hil fashioned a ring for himself and attached a tooth on the top, a false tooth from one of the trays of teeth Elsa had for her clients, the dentists."

"Leon was different from the rest of us," Marian continued. "He was a businessman. I suspect he was like my father. He set up a clothing business with Elsa while he was in the Ghetto. They bought used clothing in the Ghetto, disassembled the garments, reversed the fabrics, and then restitched them into less worn-looking garments. They smuggled the clothing outside the Ghetto and sold it for a profit," he added with a sad smile.

"Why did they leave?"

"In August 1942, after the *Aktions* began, they were able to secure life-saving jobs working for the Germans in a munitions factory, just outside the Ghetto walls. They needed to pull some strings to get the jobs," Marian added, emphasizing with a nod how precious these particular jobs had been.

I would learn that because the *Wehrmacht* branch handling munitions needed the Jewish workforce to meet their obligations, the Germans made every effort to protect these Jews — their free labor force — providing a safer environment, one with less chance of any "relocations."

"Leon was able to visit me after I left the Ghetto. And then, he didn't come anymore." The decision to make ammunition for the Germans, as distressing as it must have been, kept Leon and Hil alive until sometime before April 1943, when both Leon and Hil were deported to Treblinka and death.

For two years, between November 1940 and the summer of 1942, the family moved from one location to another within the confines of the Ghetto, escaping the initial deportations — the German *Aktions*. Certain deeply buried images should perhaps not be unearthed for the sake of enlightening others; Marian did not encourage me to envision the amply documented atrocities that the Nazis and their collaborators committed during their occupation of Warsaw. His omissions speak to his protective sensibilities. Taking care not to subject either of us to the horrors he experienced, he skipped instead to his survival outside the Ghetto, in the safety of the Polish countryside.

Marian left the Ghetto, on January 18, 1943, shortly before his thirteenth birthday, and just before the Warsaw Ghetto Uprising. He told me nothing of the escape. I had to wait some time to hear how he simply walked out of the Ghetto, just hours before the next wave of deportations and the first organized, armed resistance began.

The second uprising, climaxing in April-May, was a heroic fight to the death for the Jews remaining in the Ghetto — the Jews who anticipated, with an invigorating vengeance, the last and final deportation to Treblinka. Unlike the hundreds of Jews who knew they would be martyred in their attempts to fight their captors, Elzbieta chose to get her family and friends out of the Ghetto and into safe havens. She entrusted Marian and Eliane's family — Jacob, Joseph, and Danka — to the Polish property owner Stasio Drabich, who initially hid Marian in his own home in the outskirts of Warsaw.

"Stasio placed Joseph, Danka, and Jacob with a cousin, who lived in Praga," Marian told me. "I was with Stasio during the Warsaw Ghetto Uprising in April – May 1943, but I joined the others — in Praga — that summer."

Although he considered himself a landlord, Stasio was a well-educated man who owned an apartment house and some land. Marian wistfully described what a good cook Stasio was and how he let young Marian stay by his side, keeping him company as Marian played with and took care of Stasio's dog. Clearly, the smile on Marian's face and his soft, almost breaking voice cued the great affection Marian still felt for this man.

Over coffee at my kitchen table, late that summer afternoon a lifetime later — with a view of my back yard and Ella and LJ's previous excavating experiences — Marian gathered himself for more. Enthusiastically, he now began to tell me the particular story he wanted to relay: how he managed to escape the clutches of the Gestapo after his stay with Stasio.

"Stasio must have been distracted, 'kay?, because he didn't see the Gestapo walking up the pathway to his apartment. There was a knock at the door and Stasio let them in. I was in the back bedroom, sleeping, when they came in. I heard them enter the house and question Stasio. There was a knock on my door, and when I opened it Stasio was standing there, looking serious but calm.

'Marian, I need you to get dressed and come into the living room,' he said, rather understatedly. I pulled my pants on, grabbed one of Stasio's old shirts and walked into the living room. I stood next to Stasio as they asked me for my name and some identification, 'kay? Stasio explained that I was his friend's son, the son of a Polish friend. The men were not convinced." Marian's body tensed as he faced me now, but he did not see me as he spoke.

I could only imagine the frightened, emaciated child they must have seen with their own Jew-detecting eyes. Marian continued his story.

"They led the two of us out of the house. The Gestapo agents walked on either side of Stasio, 'kay?, and I followed them close behind. They looked like businessmen in their gray suits, 'kay?, and shiny black leather shoes. They were clean-shaven men in their twenties. I remember thinking how clean they smelled, and that they looked as though they just had haircuts. The German cross on their lapel was the only sign of their agenda.

"I saw a third agent at the wheel of their black car. I didn't know what I was going to do. I was frightened and emboldened at the same time, 'kay? I had nothing to lose. I looked to the right and saw a streetcar approaching the rear side of the car. It wasn't too far away. I tried to pace myself as it approached and as the two men put Stasio into the back seat of the car, I walked around behind it, as if I were going to enter from the other side. Without looking back I ran and jumped onto the passing trolley. I remember reaching for the handrail, not knowing if they had noticed what I had done, 'kay?, if they were going to shoot me. But they didn't realize what had happened until it was too late to stop me!" Marian's voice was exultant at these words.

Pausing, to take a deep breath and wipe the beads of sweat glistening on his forehead, Marian continued his story. "The trolley ride lasted only one stop. There were two Polish women sitting near the door when I jumped on the trolley. I saw them out of the corner of my eye. I did not look directly at them, but I saw one of them lean toward the other and mouth the word "Jew." I jumped out of the trolley and onto the street before the conductor came to collect the fare. I didn't have money on me, 'kay?, and I was sure the women would give me up. I ran through the streets, looking for a place to hide."

Marian never saw Stasio again. No one did. That day, I knew, has never left his heart.

Marian and I were sharing his relived experience and I wanted to reach out and hold the man I had called my uncle for almost four decades, but was just beginning to know. Bobby arrived home just as Marian finished his story. Glad for a chance to lighten the mood Marian now engaged his nephew in a discussion of LJ's energetic welcome. LJ, our enthusiastic puppy, was sitting at Bobby's feet, begging him to lean forward for a kiss. Marian and I both welcomed the laughter. Marian stood up and gave Bobby a warm hug. I smiled as both Marian and I returned to the safety and levity of our current lives. I needed to know how Marian's traumatic departure from Stasio was resolved, but our moments together alone were over and I busied myself making our lunch.

In the days that followed I obsessed over Marian's story, searching for clues to how Marian managed to find a safe haven after his trolley escape, and for some way of understanding Stasio, his rescuer. Stasio was a successful Polish property owner, yet he put his life on the line for another human being—someone he barely knew. I had read about how non-Jews risked their lives to save Jews during the Holocaust in Samuel P. Oliner and Pearl M. Oliner's book the *Altruistic Personality: Rescuers of Jews in Nazi Europe*. The authors noted that groups of people from the same communities faced the same situations, but that only the "rescuers" felt compelled to act. Risking their lives for others was an essential part of who they were.

Marian's story and our emerging partnership in telling it gave new form to my interest in creating a story for our granddaughter Ella. What began as a way to learn more about my husband's family, particularly Elzbieta, was becoming a relationship-changing enterprise. The more I read about the systematic extermination of European Jews, the better I could feel what Marian was allowing himself to relive in the precious accessible shreds of his life. I had no experience in my own life — or my family's — with the kinds of losses he had endured. While Marian was running from the Nazis, my own parents, who are Marian's contemporaries, danced to the music of Big Bands and enjoyed Disney's *Bambi* and Bogart and Bacall's *Casablanca* on the big screen. These were the memories they shared; I knew little of the war through their experiences. An impassioned sense of responsibility for Marian's well-being, as he slowly dared to reveal his story, overrode my shock at hearing his descriptions of life and death during the Holocaust years. I understood that oftentimes it would be essential that I simply be a compassionate sounding board for his stories of unimaginable wartime trauma.

My Sunday morning yoga class offered brief reprieve. It was a normal moment, breathing in and breathing out, yet extraordinary in its implicit safety and simplicity — breathing in and breathing out. No thoughts, no pain, no frightening anticipations and expectations, just breathe in, breathe out. Take this openness out into the day, out into your week, into your world. Namaste — as I bow to others, valuing their life and energy, I value my own. Take these thoughts with you and put them into action.

I'd entered the yoga studio, barely two hours before, pockets bulging and back packed with the disappointments, anxiety, unfulfilled expectations, and fears already filling up my week. I left in peace, feeling the air, hearing the ice crack under my fleece-crowded clogs, and willing to embrace the day's shifting wind. I slowly and carefully checked my rear-view mirror, looked to the left, looked to the right, and, confident that I would not hit or be hit, backed my car out of the parking space. I straightened the wheel to navigate the egress of the parking lot; the parking area near the yoga studio was crowded, packed with too many large SUVs registered to patrons of the neighboring diner, a popular meeting place on Sunday mornings in this affluent suburban community.

Looking ahead, watching both front corners of my mid-sized crossover, I eased through the narrow space left for me to pass through. I noticed another car that had just entered the parking lot and was

heading in my direction. I was already in the midst of my pass way —
cars parked on either side of the tightly packed path — thinking that
the other car would wait for me to exit, when I realized that the other
car was still moving, moving toward me in this constricted space, a
space already barely big enough for one car. Breathing in, breathing
out, and braking gently, I put my car into reverse and first looking to
the left, and then to the right, guided myself safely backwards with the
aid of the side-view mirror — backed out of the path of the oncoming
car. He drove past me; a man with eyes fixed straight ahead was eager
and anxious to claim the spot I had so recently left. I returned to my
enterprise — leaving the parking area through the suffocating opening
— my pockets slowly refilling with the emotional distress so peacefully
discarded earlier.

Feeling inconsequential again for the moment, my thoughts
careened — first to Marian, a mere child running through the streets
of his neighborhood, looking for safety, for recognition that his was a
valuable life, a life worth saving, and then to academic research I had
conducted years ago. My vocational interests in the development of
talent and creativity included creativity in the moral realm — remarkable
moral behavior. I had been keen on finding the link between young
children's kindnesses toward other children, and the risky self-sacrific-
ing acts of adults, of extraordinary people like Stasio Drabich, Marian's
rescuer. Exploring children's good deeds for the sake of other people in
need, my colleagues and I had unearthed the fragile roots of altruism in
simple acts of thoughtfulness, of sensitivity to the tender spark pulsing
in others.

One research participant had described a young boy sitting in his
elementary school classroom, distracted from his own work by the
child sitting near him, obviously in distress. I imagined what the teacher
didn't describe: the tears welling up in his classmate's frightened eyes
or, perhaps, overwhelmed himself by the staccato of his classmate's

marked breathing, he understood that the other child was having difficulty and that he, himself, ought to do something. I imagined the young "rescuer" reaching over and touching his classmate's shoulder, offering help.

Another teacher described "a warm, caring girl," who "was kind to everyone." This fourth grader had been acutely aware of the behavior of a new student in her class, a girl from China; she approached the newcomer and explained what was happening in the classroom by demonstrating the required tasks and introducing the English words describing her actions. This rescuer encouraged her new classmate to try new words and tasks, cheering her on as they worked together.

What I had found surprising then, what still gives me pause, was that the teachers found this type of caring behavior "extraordinary" — not typical for their students. I wondered whether today's schoolroom, with its shortage of kindnesses and generosities, is a reflection of what we — members of a community — may be losing. Are caring and principled moral behavior in short supply, risking an ungluing of our neighborhoods, our towns, our country? I soothed myself thinking about the "extraordinary" ones, the good people — good neighbors — who make a significant difference.

Holocaust rescuers, the Righteous Among the Nations, at some early moments in life must have been righteous among their family, their classmates, their neighbors, their community — doing what they considered natural: being kind, civil, and caring in their daily practice. Clearly, Marian was believing there were good people as he negotiated the familiar and unfamiliar neighborhoods of Warsaw, running from certain death and escaping into the unknown. Thinking now of my own research findings of altruism, I could imagine Marian desperately rummaging through his mind for someone he could trust, someone who had shared some kindnesses and would care about his safety.

I also envisioned his rescuer Stasio: after he lied to the Gestapo agents about Marian being a non-Jew and a friend; after he and Marian were arrested; after slowly walking between the two Gestapo agents, with Marian following behind; after he sat, or was pushed, into the back seat of the car — alongside the Gestapo — and realized that Marian had not gotten into the car; after he had watched Marian escape — jumping onto a passing trolley — knowing for certain that he would pay for all this with his own life; and after he took a breath and then let it out, feeling Marian's spark as his own and believing that this resourceful child would know where to hide. After all this, he must have smiled.

Ptasia Street No.4, Warsaw, 1939

Elzbieta knew what Benjamin was going to say before he awkwardly began the conversation she had been avoiding for days. He was going to leave. To save them both from possible harm, he was going to leave the country.

She sat down at the dining room table, in their Kredytowa Street apartment, rubbing away a smudge on the shiny new mahogany surface. Benjamin opened a bottle of wine and tried to look calm as he sat down next to her and poured both of them a hefty dose of courage. "L'chaim," he toasted, clicking his glass against hers, hoping she didn't see the tremble in his hand.

"You must be careful," she began, as if he had already revealed his plan. "You must promise me you will be careful and take care of my father."

Benjamin, looking confused, not knowing how to respond to his new bride who seemed to have read his mind and helped him — helped him make this moment easier for both of them — began to cry. "I love you. I will love you with my last breath," he said as he held Elzbieta in his arms and wept. She was stronger than he could ever be and it gave him great comfort to know that.

Elzbieta's mother Rivka had made sure that the twins were asleep in their house on Warsaw's Ptasia Street No. 4, before she allowed her husband Israel to talk to her. She could hardly believe the stories he had been telling her since the beginning of September, when Germany invaded Poland: she trusted Israel to make an intelligent decision, as he always did.

Israel had sat her down to talk about their future. He had friends outside of Warsaw who were warning him to leave. It was a matter of time before the Germans would reach Warsaw and there were still options. He had heard the horrible stories of the lists of Jewish businessmen — names gathered by the Nazis to make arrests more efficient; men were dragged from their homes and, if they resisted, were shot on the spot. "Why would they kill them unless this is what they planned to do?" Israel reasoned with Rivka, who could not believe the rumors. "We need to make a plan, so that the family will be safe. If I leave, there will be no head of the family to arrest. Adam will come with me and so will Benjamin. Leon is young enough to stay. He is a salesman, not an owner. This is what you will be able to say if they question you."

Rivka packed some warm clothes in a satchel. "Not too much," Israel had warned her. She made sure her

daughter-in-law Danka had done the same for Adam.
Elzbieta would have a more difficult time with this, she
thought to herself as she put some warm wool socks into the
pocket of the suitcase. She is still a bride, she told herself,
weeping and trying desperately to control her fears. I will
be strong and encourage her to let him go, even if I am so
frightened for them and for the rest of us.

Rivka knew that Leon would give her a difficult time
with Israel's decision to take only Adam and Benjamin, but
Israel needed Leon to stay, to help with the twins and to
keep Hil from doing something foolish. She worried about
Hil's friends, the Zionist group he was spending so much
time with at his school. Surely they wouldn't advise him to
do something to put his life at risk. If Israel thought they
should leave he would have said so. She knew Leon was
savvy enough about politics to make the right decisions.
Israel was trying to maximize their survival — maybe the
Germans will be defeated soon and Israel, Adam, and
Benjamin would be able to come back.

Rivka watched them leave from the window of her
apartment. She fought to push the thoughts out of her
mind, the thoughts that had kept her up all night — the
fear incarnating an image of her saying goodbye to her
husband for the last time.

5

Digging Deeper, Winter 2010

"He who seeks to approach his own buried past must
conduct himself like a man digging. . . . He must not be afraid
to return again and again to the same matter; to scatter it
as one scatters earth, to turn it over as one turns over soil.
For the matter itself is only a deposit, a stratum, which yields
only to the most meticulous examination what
constitutes the real treasure hidden within the earth.

– Walter Benjamin

Several months passed before I could engage Marian in a conversation revealing how and where he found refuge from the Gestapo. Much as I needed to know how the story ended, I waited till I had Marian's willing attention before I asked him to relive his flight from certain death. It was at Marian's eightieth birthday celebration, on March 7, 2010, nearly a year after Ella sat digging in my back yard, that a family celebration encouraged him toward a deeper level of revelation.

I tried to clear my head as we neared Marian's home, thinking instead of the joy we were bringing to our beloved uncle. Bobby and I reached Marian's home with our son Adam, his wife Lisa, and our precious Ella right behind us. Our older son Seth arrived directly from Manhattan some hours later.

We overwhelmed Marian with our surprise visit and the celebration began, much to his delight, with my dogs — LJ and our border collie Maggie — running into the house and greeting everyone with generous licks. Marian's tearful smile and laughter revealed how happy he was to have his entire family — his wife Carol, two sons, grandson, daughter-in-law, and my family — all under one roof, even if it was only for an afternoon. I reflected on the quiet sad moments I had shared with Marian as we revisited the Ghetto and his escape, and then took in the exuberance of the day, of the moment.

As I walked through the kitchen, with its warm walnut cabinets and linen-white walls, into the dining room, I noticed the first of several familiar paintings. The cubistic harlequin, with its large brushstrokes and dark-valued blues, startled me with the rush of memory from Elzbieta's apartment that the painting carried with it. I stood before the piece of art that Elzbieta had acquired in France years before I ever met her, and sensed the warmth of her Upper East Side home, the soft silk of her French designer scarves, and the smell of Chanel.

A handful of years before her mind began to disappear, Elzbieta had given Marian and Carol a number of paintings to fill their bare apartment walls. As I revisited each stroke on each familiar canvas, I felt embraced by Elzbieta's presence. The painting of flowers, executed with a painting knife in a dark palette of reds and black, was the one I had been moved to duplicate decades ago. I remembered how Elzbieta had encouraged me to experiment with my painting knife, exploring the possibilities of capturing the essence of an object, like the broad petals of a flower, without all the unnecessary details. Each of these paintings, with all of its evidences of a life once lived, had survived and found a place in Marian's daily milieu. Entering Marian's home now I was unprepared for encountering these buried memories, these reminders of my own encounters with Elzbieta.

Sitting to the right of Bobby at the dining room table, I surveyed the bookshelves surrounding the fireplace at the end of the room; the eggshell-white shelves served as guardians of family photographs as well as precious objets d'art. Noticing a picture of Marian's father, Israel,

I mentioned to Carol how much Marian and their son Marc resembled Israel. Marian got out of his chair, went over to a shelf, and brought a small, unnoticed picture to the table. He sat down next to Bobby and pointed to the picture, a black and white image of Marian's mother Rivka and the other women in her family.

"This is my mother Rivka, her two sisters — I have forgotten their names — and my Grandma Wilde," he explained. Marian's mother, who must have been in her teens, stood behind her two seated sisters, also likely in their teens or early twenties. Rivka's wavy dark hair was pulled back and tied behind her head, and she was the only one to have a hint of a smile. Her mother stood to Rivka's left, one hand holding one of the seated sisters' wrists, the other bent behind her back. This was the first time Bobby had seen an image of his grandmother and her family. Their long dresses and laced-up black boots made them all seem far away in time and place.

We were stunned. Until this moment neither Bobby nor I had known that his Grandmother Rivka had two sisters: We learned now that one sister had moved to Switzerland before the war and survived Hitler's ferocious murdering spree. The other was in the Ghetto with Marian and perished, along with her husband and children.

I was struck by the familiarity of Rivka's image, but knew I had never seen her photograph. I searched the image with my artist eyes, looking for cheekbones and eyes replicated in her descendants. Yet this was not the resemblance I had already perceived. I was moved to tears when I realized. The source of the similarity was a painting, now hanging in my bedroom beside my bed — a painting once owned by Elzbieta.

The portrait had hung on Elzbieta's living room wall, to the right of her Danish-Modern sofa. Because the wall behind the painting jutted out slightly into the room — perhaps hiding ducts or pipes — the painting appeared to reach out into the viewer's space. I didn't need physical confrontation by the beautiful face the famed Polish artist Tade

Styka had captured in his tender rendering of his model; I was drawn to its expression of peaceful resignation as soon as I entered the room. I never questioned who the model had been, sensing that Elzbieta had also been drawn to her tender beauty. I realized, in this moment at Marian's, that the portrait conveyed an essence of Rivka's own features and tenderness. Elzbieta had seen that too.

Rivka had two brothers as well. I would eventually learn about one of them who had immigrated to the United States before the war. After the war, when Marian came to the states and contacted his uncle, the man was reluctant to speak to him, believing Marian wanted financial help and not simply family ties. Angered by his uncle's coldness, Marian never had another chance to get to know his mother's family.

At Marian's table I held the tiny faded black and white photograph in my hand. What would it be like to have so little left to help remember what had once been a large family? Marian returned to his seat without me noticing he had left the room. Carol and the others had slipped away unnoticed as well, talking quietly amongst themselves in the next room. We were sitting together talking, Marian and I, when Carol came back into the room and sat at the table several seats away from the two of us. I thought it was strange that she didn't sit next to us. I dismissed the distance as a way for her to give Marian and me some space to talk, a degree of privacy, and, at the same time, an opportunity for her to listen to what Marian had to say. It was at this quiet, intimate moment that Marian took several pictures out of a slim clear-plastic folder. He looked pleased.

"This is me," he said with delight, "and my brother Menache, 'kay?"

I looked at Marian, who was smiling at the tiny photograph — an old, shiny black and white Kodak image, creased and worn along its deckled edges. I had never seen a picture of Menache and was taken by the fact that though the twin boys were dressed alike, they were not identical twins. Marian was blond and muscular, Menache was anemically thin with a broader forehead, darker hair, and more sallow complexion. They were nine years old in the picture, and playing at acrobatics in their matching light-colored khaki shorts and dark t-shirts. Marian was slightly taller and appeared the stronger one — supporting his brother on his own shoulders as he looked out at the photographer, smiling. The picture permitted a deeper look into the childhood captured in one brief moment in time. The two were full of life, full of promise for a privileged future together. In just one year they would lose their home and sense of security entirely. In three years, their mother and their cellular bond; Menache would die three years later as well, in 1942, and Marian would feel the empty space in his life forever. Until this day, this instant, Marian's twinship had been an abstraction. The photograph made Marian's loss agonizingly real.

By the end of the year, Marian would receive a newer, clearer treasured image of the two of them. I enlarged the fragile two-inch by three-inch photograph, strengthened the contrast, and printed it on eight-by-ten photo paper. Marian's reaction was joyful: "Sue, looking at this image I can remember exactly when that picture was taken! It was the summer before the war and my father had rented a house in the countryside. My mother went to the spa with her friends and family and we, Menache and I, had so much fun. We spent the entire summer away from the city and didn't return until the end of August."

I realized what they encountered within just weeks of their return, in September of 1939. "We had just come home and were preparing to start school — home from a wonderful summer — 'kay?, when the Germans marched into Warsaw." Marian would mark the end of his blissful childhood, the end of playful poses with smiling faces, with chilling images of war. It would take later conversations before Marian would reveal that the large picture I had sent him had — beyond the joy he expressed — of course also saddened him, terribly.

Removing another fragile picture from its protective case, on that day of his eightieth birthday, Marian smiled down at the image.

"And here we are with my mother, 'kay?, and my brother Hil," Marian chuckled, pointing to Rivka, wrapped in a long striped bathrobe. She stood straight, without a smile, looking almost annoyed at the photographer, as she held the front of her robe together. Her hands were wrapped around her waist, as if the wind would blow the robe open at any moment. Hil stood to her left in a buttoned dress coat, the twins in front of her, grinning broadly. I wondered who had taken the photograph. Israel? Elzbieta? Or perhaps Leon, the one brother for whom I had no image.

Both pictures had been taken before the war at Ciechocinek, a town in north central Poland. This spa town on the Vistula River is still known today for its local saline springs and legendary therapeutic "cures" for cardiovascular, respiratory, and nervous system maladies. In the 1930s, when Marian and his family vacationed there, the spa had luscious gardens and beautiful accommodations for guests. During the war, the town served as a military hospital and a health resort for German citizens.

"Here's a picture of Elsa with Benjamin," Marian said softly with a smile acknowledging my awareness of Elzbieta's first husband. The tiny photograph of Benjamin — standing straight and almost Elzbieta's height — within a group of people bundled up in winter coats, required some assistance to grasp. Benjamin stood to Elzbieta's left, Israel to her right, amongst a group Marian described as co-workers in their business enterprises. The photograph must have been taken several years before the war.

"Father had taken Elzbieta, Benjamin, and Adam — there, standing to Benjamin's left — for a vacation along with some of the other workers. I was not there," Marian added, as he pointed to each family member.

I hadn't recognized Israel in the tiny photograph. "I didn't know Israel wore a mustache. That kind of mustache," I added, before Marian could respond.

"Yes, he wore a mustache then," Marian said, turning his face away. I could see that both Israel and Benjamin sported a toothbrush mustache — a style originating in the United States decades before the war. After the war the style fell from favor; it became associated with Hitler, earning the nickname "Hitler mustache."

The once-fashionable mustaches also reminded me of a photograph I found in a box of Elzbieta's mementos — a small snapshot of a mustachioed man walking arm-in-arm with Elzbieta through the streets of Warsaw. Marian hadn't recognized the miniscule face in the original photograph. I had brought an enlarged version with me; perhaps Marian could identify a larger image of this "mystery man."

"Do you know who this is?" I asked Marian, retrieving the now eight-by-ten photograph from my satchel.

"Yes, of course! I recognize the hairline and the forehead. It's Benjamin," Marian said, with satisfaction at remembering a face he hadn't seen since age nine.

The image of Benjamin, much clearer than the group shot Marian held in his hands, seemed much older to me. I could only imagine what had transpired in the time between the two pre-war photos. Elzbieta had made sure both pictures of Benjamin survived.

"I didn't know you had these pictures — Bobby never mentioned them," I said, speaking calmly, hoping to gather information without annoying Marian or frightening him into silence. I would learn later that day that Bobby had never seen Marian's precious handful of family photographs.

"Elsa gave them to me after the war," Marian said, acknowledging Elzbieta's efforts to salvage what she could of Marian's privileged and happy early childhood. "I don't know how she kept them all those years," he said, a wistful softness in his voice.

"She had so many pictures," he added. "After the war, she put together a book, a book that was published."

"What kind of book? What were the pictures of? " I asked him. I was incredulous. How could something so important be forgotten or kept secret all these years?

"She was working with a committee after the war, 'kay? Actually a handful of people, friends of hers. They gathered pictures, mostly photographs taken during the war. They bought them from people on the streets of Warsaw. Many were taken by German soldiers — their trophies of war," Marian said, trying to explain the book. "I remember so many of the photographs in Elsa's apartment. She would go out into the city and come back excited at finding and buying another picture for the album."

"What was the album for? What were they going to do with it?" I asked, as Marian stood up from his seat.

"Carol, where is the book?" Marian turned to his wife who was sitting near us, but not too close.

"I don't know, somewhere. I haven't seen it recently," she answered, then continued eating her dessert. I couldn't understand why she was so nonchalant, seemingly uninterested. Wasn't this important?

Marian left the dining room and returned a few moments later. He brought a book back with him and placed it on the table. Its binding torn and separating, and its once-black cover faded to a charcoal gray, it had a curious title. Across the front, huge letters announced its contents: *Extermination of Polish Jews: Album of Pictures*. My heart stopped at the sight.

I opened the book with immense respect, and gratefulness for Marian's trust. Marian showed me that the description of its contents and introduction were presented in six different languages: Yiddish, Polish, Russian, Hebrew, French, and English. The book was published in 1945, in Lodz, Poland, when relatively little was known of the magnitude of the genocide perpetrated upon the European Jews. The album contains more than two hundred and fifty black and white

photographs, with a short introduction by Polish historian Philip
Friedman, and a dedication to the partisan movements by the editor
Gershon Taffet, head of the Photographic Division of the Central Jewish
Historical Committee in Poland. The images show Jewish settlements
at the beginning of the German occupation, life and death inside the
ghettos, and the atrocities committed in both forced labor and extermination camps. The photographs were graphic, heart-wrenching to look
at, let alone analyze. I felt almost dizzy, trying to focus on the pictures
and descriptions Marian had chosen to show me.

As Marian began to thumb through the book, I turned away.
I found myself increasingly unprepared for the images of starving
children and Nazi soldiers tormenting Jews. I glimpsed one picture
depicting two German soldiers cutting off the hair, beards, and side
curls of two Jews, who stood in passive obedience — their tallit hanging
from their shirts and sweaters. I could not find words for the images
before me. Marian pointed to one picture after another, identifying the
pictures he remembered Elzbieta contributing to the collection. We had
crossed a line into openness, into daring, Marian and I. I hoped to keep
my balance as I began to comprehend the incomprehensible. This was
our family's life.

"Warsaw had two ghettos," Marian spoke now. "One was called the
small one and the other was called the big one. We were in the big one
and to get to it you had to cross a bridge, 'kay?" He pointed to the
photograph of a wooden footbridge, with crowds of people making
their way, this way and that way, across to the other section of a ghetto
at Lodz; the empty, forbidden street between the two ghetto sections lay
below it. The image had sparked Marian's memory of a similar footbridge in the Warsaw Ghetto. I was grateful that he turned the pages
quickly, as he sought specific pictures he remembered seeing in
Elzbieta's Warsaw apartment, after the war. I turned my gaze from the
emaciated infants, their heads looking too large for their limp bony

bodies and stomachs swollen from the Natzis' strategy of starvation.

"Elsa said they got together at night and talked about the photographs they had seen," he continued. He spoke more openly, more freely than any time before.

"The whole committee was maybe four or five people. I think a couple of Elsa's friends pulled her into it, 'kay? I never attended their meetings. I actually got this copy when I was in London after the war. She sent it to me and she had one too. They didn't give themselves credit for the book. It was their responsibility just to put it together, 'kay?" Marian spoke now with unexpected enthusiasm. The postwar documentation spurred him on, at last.

"There weren't many books published. For one thing, they didn't have the ability. They didn't have many printed because they had to pay for it out of their own pockets. It certainly wasn't a big seller, or anything like that, 'kay?" Marian said, with a little sarcastic chuckle, trying to recall what he remembered about the book.

"This is one of the pictures Elsa bought, I know it, 'kay?" Marian said, his voice rising in volume along with the certainty of his memory.

I saw an image of the Ghetto wall and thought about the Jews, about Marian and Elzbieta, isolated behind barbed wire and bricks. "This is probably the Jewish side. By the look of it, it was taken from the inside, 'kay? I can tell — on the other side you can see trees.

"They wanted to make sure the world knew what happened," he added, looking for another picture of the Ghetto he wanted me to see. The images were not mere textbook documentation of Holocaust atrocities. They were the first time I had experienced images of dead, dying, and humiliated Jews without some distance, without the muffling and protecting effects of observing strangers. Suddenly I was forced to acknowledge my own proximity to these events, through my husband's beloved family. This was the heritage of our children, our grandchildren. I had no idea what more I could and would bring myself to read, to envision, in helping Marian fully reveal his story for our family.

Heightened by his unexpected voyage into the Ghetto, Marian's enthusiasm for showing and telling created an atmosphere of exhilaration — a contagious mood tempered by the layer of dread elicited by the images of ravaged Jews. I tried to ignore the album's images of shoes and eyeglasses piled in heaps as detritus, the mounds of corpses rendered alien by their reduction to skin stretched over bones. I forced myself to focus on the words in the book's introduction. Where were the names of people who created this unusual collection? I found no names of the members of the "Central Jewish Historical Committee in Poland." They were an unnamed handful of survivors who needed to take action, needed to gather the evidence before it was lost — proof that human beings could do this to one another.

Marian carefully put the book back in the white cardboard box that had protected it for all these years. He looked up at Carol, who was still sitting, quietly, on the other side of the table. "I don't need to hold on to this any longer," he said, pushing the box away from him, toward the middle of the table. Carol waved her hand, suggesting both her agreement with Marian's conclusion and her eagerness to rid the house and their lives of these memories. I understood now. Carol's apparent indifference to our conversation had been her way of avoiding the book and what it represented to Marian.

As I sat back to collect my thoughts, and reviewed the preparations for this visit that I had made earlier in the day, I asked Marian if we could talk further. Were still more questions alright after such an emotional time? He consented. I needed to start with a slow, fact-driven conversation, to focus both of us and yet engage him in this unanticipated need to share. I took out some of the papers I had brought with me and put one particular document on the table.

"Marian," I began, "I did some research regarding testimony recognizing someone as a rescuer, a non-Jewish rescuer of Jews. The Yad

Vashem website has a submission form that I downloaded. It requests a written story of how someone saved your life," I said, moving the form toward Marian. I told him how I had learned about Yad Vashem, the Jewish memorial to the Righteous Among the Nations, from Samuel and Pearl Oliner's book about rescuers. I described how a commission examines each testimony and is responsible for granting this title, and how the names of those individuals who are recognized are commemorated on the Mount of Remembrance in Jerusalem.

"The 'Righteous' come from forty-four countries, can you imagine?" I added. They are Christians from all denominations — religious and agnostic. The men and women, from all lifestyles, are alike in their humanity and the courage they displayed standing up for their moral principles." I handed the submission form to Marian.

"I know about Yad Vashem," he responded. "I was there when I went to Israel years ago, but I cannot name someone who was compensated — who was paid for his help."

I didn't know how to respond. Marian had never mentioned paying Stasio for his help.

"When we were outside the Ghetto, there is only one person who helped us — who was not paid, 'kay? Stasio Drabich helped me because we had a relationship."

Marian had forgotten telling me about Stasio's help. "There were others outside the Ghetto?" I asked, hoping he would remember names.

"Yes, I can't remember names, but we paid them. We had gold and we paid them," he said.

"I wonder if that really makes a difference, Marian," I answered. "At some moment, money couldn't have been motivation enough for them to put their lives on the line. I want you to know I searched for someone named Stanislaw Drabich or Drabik and was able to find some information about Stasio, or at least someone I think was Stasio," I said as I looked through my fistful of papers. I handed Marian the document describing "Stanislaw Drabik's" arrest and subsequent death at Gusen work camp.

With contempt for his actions, the Nazis must have labeled Stasio "a helper of Jews" and imprisoned him. The Polish document I had found seemed stark proof of Stasio's arrest and death: "A Austria: Mauthausen / Gusen Concentration Camp Death" — Stanislaw Drabik, a Pole, born February, 1, 1902, in Warsaw, was arrested and taken to Gusen — arriving in September, 1944. Stasio died on March 12, 1945." Marian sat very still, the piece of paper in his lap, as he looked upon the words printed before him and tried to articulate their significance. "Yes, this was him," was all he whispered.

The two main camps, Mauthausen and Gusen I, were the only two camps in the whole of Europe to be labeled as "Grade III" camps: they were intended to be the toughest camps for the "Incorrigible Political Enemies of the Reich." Unlike many other concentration camps, intended for all categories of prisoners, Mauthausen / Gusen was used mostly for extermination, through labor, of the intelligentsia — the educated people and members of the higher social classes in countries subjugated by the Nazi regime.

"Yes, this was Stasio," Marian said again, as he pointed to the date of arrest and the year of birth. "He was around my father's age. I know this because he knew my father before the war. He actually helped my father when he needed money," Marian said, clearly eager to tell this story and not delve further into the painful confirmation of Stasio's death.

"My father, before he made money from his successful businesses, 'kay? He needed money for his first venture. Stasio lent him money. Even though, as a Catholic, money-lending was against his beliefs, he lent my father money, 'kay? He did it because my father was a Jew, not a Catholic." Marian laughed as he explained the business relationship and the humor he found in the way Stasio circumvented his religious conviction.

"They became friends, good friends. In fact, when we were in the Ghetto, Elsa sat all of us down and asked who we thought could help us get out. Who was outside, a Pole whom we could trust? That is how we went to Stasio for help," Marian said, explaining the relationship with Stasio.

"Elsa got in touch with him. We didn't have his telephone number or anything. She found him somehow, and arranged that I leave the Ghetto. Sometime in January of 1943, 'kay? I left the Ghetto and in April of 1943 was the uprising. I left the Ghetto and he agreed that I could come to his apartment," Marian said, taking a deep breath as if gearing himself up for the whole story. I still didn't know the exact circumstances of Marian's escape from the Ghetto and this was the moment I had waited for.

"How did you leave?" I asked, hoping for more information than Marian had voluntarily revealed.

"Elsa knew we had no choice," he continued. "We had to leave, 'kay? We had to leave certain death at the hands of the Nazis and take the risks of life on the Aryan side. She made her contacts within the Ghetto aware of her need: to get me out safely. I don't think she had any idea how the escape would play out.

"I had been anxious and melancholy since they took my mother and brother three months before, 'kay? I didn't question Elsa when she told me what to do. The place where we were living, the Holiest Virgin Mary church on Leszno Street, was crammed. It was housing more people than its bursting walls could comfortably tolerate. I was eager to leave the confines of the church that day, even if it meant going out into the cold. . . .

"It was a wintry day in the middle of January, 'kay? A light bulb broke at a guard station near the gate about one-half mile from our quarters. The security guard requested an electrician who just happened to have been close to Elsa's network of outside contacts." Marian smiled as he nodded in my direction. I understood how the people you knew and the money you managed to hold on to could decide life or death.

" 'Marian,' Elsa said carefully, 'I need you to go with my friend to fix the light. You are to do exactly what he tells you to do.' I had listened to Elsa's directions and then repeated them, several times, at her request, 'kay?, before I returned to the book of poetry I read repeatedly, night and day.

"I remember Elsa rummaging through my bundle of clothes, looking for something, something presentable. I waited on the street, just as she told me, 'kay?, keeping busy with my book of poetry. I was waiting for a man with a ladder to show up. He came by me, walking toward the gate, 'kay?, and I stood up, picked up the speed of his gait, and gave him a nod and a smile, just as I was told to do. We continued down the street, toward the gate. I was not sure of exactly what would happen. 'It is better this way,' Elsa had warned me.

"When a German soldier stopped us and asked what we were doing with a toolbox and ladder, the electrician showed the officer his papers and explained the nature of his work and the orders to fix the light. 'Who is he?' the soldier asked, pointing to me. 'He is my assistant,' the electrician answered, 'kay?, as if it was obvious what I was doing there.

"I held the ladder as the electrician took his time assessing the malfunctioning light. I passed him tools when he pointed to something he needed from the toolbox, 'kay? I remember it being bitter cold, but I didn't care. The cold air calmed me down, helped me shift my focus from thinking about possible outcomes to what was necessary: keeping warm.

'I need a new light bulb,' the electrician told the soldier. 'I don't have the right one here. I will have to go get one.'

"The soldier acquiesced, letting both of us walk out the gate. I imagine that the electrician returned some time later with the light bulb, only the light bulb," Marian said with a chuckle.

"Once I was out of sight of the soldiers guarding the gate, I headed in the direction Elsa had described to me and made me memorize. I had no idea what lay ahead of me. It had to be that way.

"When I reached my destination, an apartment house on Wolska Street, I knocked on the door of the apartment Elsa had made me memorize, not knowing who and what I would find. Stasio opened the door," Marian stated with a huge smile on his face.

It seemed like such a simple plan for Marian's escape to the Aryan side, but I could only imagine how frightened Elzbieta must have been to let him go alone. Each day they would have heard stories of people leaving the Ghetto, then getting caught and killed.

"The day I showed up," Marian continued, "Stasio greeted me, got me a plate of food, and showed me what to do, where to stay, and how to feed his dog. In back of the building he had a farm where he was growing onions. He had a side business selling onions wholesale. I was there for a short time, maybe for a month or two — I can't remember exactly how long I stayed — and then one of his tenants got wind of my visit and asked Stasio what I was doing there. Stasio suspected she would turn him in," Marian said, trying to shed light on the threat he felt for his own safety, even in the company of Stasio.

"Since Stasio was the landlord, he had the authority to issue documents stating that we lived there, at this building. Stasio knew a priest, 'kay? And the local priest would give you a baptismal certificate. Elsa would get Bobby's father Joseph and his family — Danka and Jacob — out too, but I didn't know. She found a way to get them out, got them identification as a non-Jew, and then they went on to a safe house. It wasn't difficult to get out of the Ghetto at that time. All you needed to do was bribe someone. The difficult part was getting papers and finding someone to hide you or give you shelter without questioning whether you were a Jew.

"Stasio's priest got baptismal certificates for Elsa's other friends too.

He got us all identification saying that we were gentiles and we lived at Stasio's apartment house, 'kay? I had identification saying I was Marian Rudski. Elsa was Elzbieta Rejewska.

"Elsa would show up occasionally and when she recommended some of her friends, Stasio was very willing to help. He was a patriot, a true patriot. Not so much a Jew lover, but a Polish patriot," Marian said, trying to explain Stasio's motivation to help Elzbieta's friends as well as her family.

I asked him if Stasio was involved with the Polish underground. He didn't know.

"If he was, he wouldn't have told me," Marian said, making sure I understood the clandestine nature of the organization. "He helped save so many of Elsa's friends. That was how it happened, how he was suspected and finally caught."

"Elsa had two very good friends," he continued. "They were so close, we used to eat there and sleep there, 'kay? The man was a banker before the war and his wife was a professor of languages. She spoke perfect German, English, and Polish and didn't look Jewish, 'kay?, but she had Jewish expressions. Elsa got them out and got a place for them from Stasio. The woman was very intelligent and she couldn't sit still at home. She had to find a job, so she found work outside of Warsaw. It was a good position. I think she was translating for the Germans, from German to English.

"Nora, Nora Goldman was her name, 'kay? How did I remember that? Nora, Nora, I wouldn't forget her. She was childless. She treated me like a kid!" Marian said, as if still annoyed after all these years. "They couldn't afford to do things, but every time I would come she would have cakes for me, cookies for me — she didn't know what to do for me, 'kay?"

Marian continued the story, after a moment's reflection, smiling for someone he had cared for — and who had cared about him — so many years ago. "They found out she was Jewish so they arrested her, 'kay? Because she had a baptismal certificate and a place of registration with Stasio's address, they came to arrest him. That is how it all happened."

Marian, caught up in the retelling of his and Stasio's arrest, lowered his voice, as if he were too preoccupied with the imagery, with replaying the scene. "I happened to have come from the country—I was staying with him for a day or two and I was there when they arrested him," Marian repeated, his voice barely audible.

"I was staying with Stasio for a short visit because I couldn't stay in the house he had found for me. The people were suspicious of me and I was frightened. Stasio was going to place me in another location. I was supposed to be there temporarily, until I found another place. I wasn't supposed to be there very long, but I loved staying with him and his dog," Marian said, his thoughts drifting off as if considering the endless outcomes that could have played out.

Marian sat very still, looking down at his hands resting on the linen tablecloth. He looked up at me with a start—as if I had called his name—and then continued the story, with new urgency, of how he had escaped from the Gestapo that day of the trolley car.

"What happened? Stasio took me to a concert on Sunday, and after the performance he took me for tea and pastry in a restaurant. That was all you ate there!" Marian said, with his hands up in the air, emphasizing the restaurant's specialized menu—a bill of fare for its wealthy clientele.

"After the restaurant he took me to visit his cousins who lived in another one of his apartment buildings. It was a small building on the other side of the Vistula, in Praga. It was on the other side of Warsaw. Stasio took me there, didn't tell me a word. He didn't tell me anything about his cousins. Then we went home and the next morning was when the Gestapo came and arrested him; arrested both of us, 'kay?

"Elsa was in the village working as a nurse, but I didn't know where, deliberately. I told her not to tell me. If they got hold of me and asked, 'Where's your sister?' I would tell them, 'I don't know,' " Marian said, explaining his ignorance of Elzbieta's whereabouts.

"When I was running from the Gestapo, after jumping off the trolley car and running through the streets of Warsaw, I remembered Stasio's cousins, 'kay? I remember thinking it was the only place I could go. If he hadn't taken me there, if Stasio hadn't taken me there, I would not have known where to go," he added, reliving his decision-making.

"Oh, I knew what to do. The only thing to do would have been to go to the Jewish cemetery and hide there because you had no place to go. No place, 'kay?

"So I decided to go back to Stasio's cousins. I don't remember their name. I wish I could. His cousin had a wife and a child — they were a nice Polish family. When I got there I found out they had Joseph and his family hiding behind a double wall in the attic! 'kay? They also had a goat in the attic, above their apartment. Can you imagine, a goat? They were all living there, in the attic — Joseph, Jacob, Danka, and the goat!" Marian began to laugh at the memory. "Feeding the goat was their excuse for bringing food up to the attic." I was stunned at this news too. To survive, my husband's family had hidden in an attic with a goat.

"I was in that attic for a year and a half. Imagine that, 'kay? They were very nice people, the cousins, and we paid them for their help," he said with a slow, deliberate voice, perhaps now questioning the importance of their being compensated. "We paid them for their help."

"If we were to be dropped today in Warsaw, I would find my way to their house," Marian said, reflecting on the story he had just told me. I asked him if he wanted to go back to Warsaw, for a visit. "Yes," Marian answered, after a hesitation. "I would go back to Warsaw now, just to walk those streets."

Warsaw Ghetto, 1943

Elzbieta pushed her face against the cold windowpane of the old church on Leszno Street. She tried to catch a glimpse of Marian as he sat waiting on the steps below exactly as planned — waiting and watching as he hunched over his book. Observing him through the distortions of the old rippled glass made him look so young, so vulnerable.

They had made the decision together, all of them, she thought to herself, as she recalled Marian and their friend Joseph and his family stealing some time to talk in the shadows of the dark damp church. Marian would leave first. The help he would get was assured. The rest of them would have to take their chances, but young Marian must get out safely.

She saw the electrician approaching before Marian picked his head up from the worn pages of poetry. She wanted to scream out for him to remember what she had told him, but she couldn't. He wouldn't have heard her anyway as he slowly got up and picked up the cadence of the electrician's gait. In a moment, she could barely see him. He was out of sight. She felt the pain of hunger mix with her nausea. He will be safe, she said to herself, more a prayer than a belief.

Elzbieta turned away from the window and focused on the crowds of huddled friends and strangers sitting and sleeping in the church's dimly lit room. She had assured Marian she would be fine, that she would follow him shortly, that he would have a safe place to live. How could she have promised something she only prayed would be true? There were so many uncontrollable possibilities — so many things could go wrong, so many people to depend on. Elzbieta fought back images of Marian being arrested, tortured, or shot on the spot. She swallowed hard as her hand rested, almost instinctively, on the capsule of cyanide she had pinned into the soft folds of her camisole; she was prepared to take her own life if the Nazis captured her.

For their own safety, they had all needed to leave their residences after the last roundup in September — two families forced to join others in crowded unsanitary conditions at a residence close to the workshop. The church had seemed like a safe place to stay, living alongside the converts. Nonetheless, Elzbieta knew it was just a matter of time before someone would come for them — before the Germans or their hateful collaborators would come for Toebbens's and Schultz's workers.

Leaving the clinic after what seemed like an endless day, Elzbieta walked along the desperate streets until she reached Nora's apartment. Nora would understand what she was feeling and offer comfort without making her label her fears. She knew that her good friend, who loved Marian almost as much as she did, would help her get through the night. They wouldn't have word of Marian until tomorrow — wouldn't know until the morning if Marian had made his way to safety.

Elzbieta found Nora sitting with some friends and made her way to their small inviting group. Forcing a smile as she sat down, Elzbieta felt herself go limp as Nora put an arm around her and whispered, "He'll be fine, our little boy will be fine."

Elzbieta tried to envision Marian's sweet face. He would be thirteen in two months — hardly a little boy. The need to survive had stolen his childhood. Yet despite his swagger and fearless imitation of adulthood, Marian's essence was still ingenuous, still hopeful. She ached with hunger, but could not eat the bread she had saved from her lunch.

Elzbieta put her head on Nora's lap and lulled herself to sleep humming a sweet sentimental love song someone was singing — someone far away. She imagined Benjamin holding her in his arms as they danced — it seemed so long ago. She tried to envision the location; was it her wedding? She couldn't tell. She couldn't even make out Benjamin's features or feel the heat of his body — the intoxicating warmth that had once overwhelmed her. Giving into the dizzying loss of time, place, and feeling, Elzbieta relished the carefree safety of her dream.

6

Reliving the *Aktions* of 1942

"At a word of command we got underway.
And then, to our dismay, we came face to face with stark reality.
There were railroad cars, empty railroad cars,
waiting to receive us. It was a bright, hot summer day.
It seemed to us that the sun itself rebelled against this injustice.
What had our wives, children and mothers done to deserve this?
Why all this? The beautiful, bright, radiant sun
disappeared behind the clouds as if loath to look down
upon our suffering and degradation."

– Jankiel Wiernik

I had Marian's undivided attention on that remarkable day of his eightieth birthday. I remember weighing my need to ask questions — to encourage him to fill gaps in my understandings — and the responsibility I felt for this dear man's well-being. I needed to be sensitive in what I was asking him to relive. Ella and Bobby and the others were still talking quietly in the next room.

Afraid to move, to break the spirit as Marian shared his imagery, I waited for him to lead me to a context begging for details of people, of places, of moments. It was during the pause in Marian's conjurings that I chanced delving into memories I knew might be difficult for him to unearth. I mentioned the conversation I'd had with Bobby's cousin Eliane the previous week. Marian smiled and mentioned she had telephoned to wish him a happy birthday. He suspected I had something to do with the call. . . .

Eliane had sounded happy that I asked her for help with the family tree. She was eager to provide names of her mother's family members — the ancestors she shared with my husband Bobby. As the conversation drifted to a family update and then to Marian, Eliane mentioned the incident on the boat — that emotional exchange that left both Marian and Eliane gun-shy at later family gatherings. She told me she still wanted to speak to Marian about the war but was now afraid to confront him. She needed to know how the Germans could arrest her mother and grandmother — how they had not been protected like everyone else. I hadn't known that Eliane's mother Danka had been selected for deportation to Treblinka and had managed to survive, but her grandmother Ytel had not been so fortunate. Eliane knew that Marian at age twelve might not have known the story, but she had a need to ask him.

"Marian, I need to ask you something," I said, as I continued my inquiries. "Eliane told me of the day the Nazis took her mother and grandmother. She believes the question she asked you that time on the boat had something to do with that day. She still regrets distressing you, yet the question haunts her," I added, hoping to explain my own invasive questioning.

I looked at Marian and saw a face I did not recognize — its features frozen in a frightening grimace. Marian was trying to manage a safe reaction to my question. I had no choice but to be still, holding my breath and carefully choosing my words.

"I don't know if you even know what happened," I said, trying to slowly back away from the moment. "I'll just tell you what she told me, and you can let me know if it's the truth or not, or if you don't know." Marian managed a nod in my direction.

I repeated Eliane's story to Marian — the story of Danka and Ytel's arrest, the story that had become Eliane's own nightmare as she sought understanding.

In a hushed voiced, with her eyes closed tight to hold back the horrific images, Danka had told Eliane what happened so long ago:

"The Gestapo came for us, took us away, your grandmother and me," Danka began. "We knew what they wanted, where they were taking us: to the death side. Elzbieta and I had saved ourselves, so many times, with a smile and a look. I smiled, I looked, and I hoped it would save us. They left us alone and told us to wait. Your grandmother was so frightened. I tried to comfort her. 'We are together,' I said, in a whisper, holding your grandmother with all my might.

"A German officer got out of his car and walked over to us. He took my face in his hand and asked me my name. Danielle, I answered and smiled, fearing he could hear my heart beating, beating so fast. 'A pretty girl with a pretty name,' he said and asked me the question that still rings in my ears: 'What is a pretty girl doing here?' I didn't know what to answer, how to answer him.

"'You will run,' he told me. 'Run when I shout *Raus*.' I nodded, not understanding, but needing to respond. Your grandmother held her hands to her face, to keep herself from screaming — from calling for me, from risking my freedom, my life.

"A few minutes later he looked at me and said '*Raus*.' I couldn't move. He said it again, this time as a throaty demand, '*Raus!*'

"I ran. I didn't look back — I couldn't bear to look at her. I kept hearing Elzbieta's voice in my head, telling me over and over again that I must do what I have to do to survive. I ran to our safe place and waited for Elzbieta, for Joseph, for Papa. I never saw my mother again. They took her to Treblinka. They took your grandmother Ytel just as they took my beautiful brother Leon, his Hanna, and little boy. The soldier saved my life, not my mother's, and I never looked back."

"It was September 7, 1942, a day I cannot forget," Danka added with a sigh as she wiped at the tears streaming down her cheeks.

Marian had been sitting back in his chair. It was an unusual position for him, given his difficulty hearing, his characteristic leaning into conversations to facilitate the perception of sounds. I managed a simple question: "Marian, do you know if this is what happened?"

Marian's face was turned to his left, away from me. His head jolted back when I addressed him, as if he had just been hit across his face. With a shudder, he softly mouthed the words that sent me spinning. "Oh, I know when that happened. Yes, yes, it is true. I was there."

"You were there?" I must have stammered, because Marian looked at me as though I wasn't making sense. "You were there," I repeated. "But, how?" It was the tenderest of moments.

"It was called the 'selection,'" Marian now told me, collecting himself and his thoughts. Even people who worked for the Germans, the people they needed, were sometimes siphoned off for 'resettlement.' If they needed a thousand or two thousand to send to the camp, they would get Jews together and segregate them outdoors in the streets." He was referring to the *Aktions*, the selections that began in the summer of 1942. Initially Jews who worked in German factories were safe. Eventually even these protected workers were rounded up and sent to Treblinka.

"How Danka felt at that moment is beyond my understanding," Marian added. "I could not see her from where I stood. But it's true. We were at the same segregation, the only thing is Danka's father and her brother were on one side and Danka and her mother were on the other. As a woman, she was wanted for the camp." I wasn't sure I understood him correctly but hesitated to stop him to ask.

"In my case they wanted children and I was, in '42, twelve years old. The person I worked for, as a messenger boy at Toebbens, saved me. My mother and my brother were at Toebbens too. Their segregation took place one day and ours was the next. There were two separate streets — we assembled there and then the selection for deportation took place.

When my turn came, this Jewish woman spoke up. She was a German Jew and spoke perfect German. She even looked German, 'kay? — she was more German than Jewish. She once told me, 'I don't know why I'm a Jew. I didn't know I was Jewish. My father was Jewish. My mother wasn't Jewish,' Marian said with a slight laugh, trying to keep himself focused. This German Jewish woman shouted out in German, 'He is my messenger boy, I need him!' I was there with Elsa. We were sent back to work." He was silent for a moment, as if this was enough information to share.

"What Danka went through is true, 'kay?" Marian began again. "And that's when they lost their mother. Can you imagine that? Their mother was taken away and Joseph and Jacob were let go — all right in front of them. Can you imagine? For days Danka couldn't sleep." Marian's voice trailed off. He looked down, folding his hands in his lap.

Marian sat silently with me now, engrossed by his own memories and the story Danka had shared with her own child, Eliane. I could not halt the sounds and images I imagined: Marian's own close encounter with death, and the German soldier shouting for Danka to run. I imagined the German Jewess studying Marian's terrified face and making her fateful decision. I also imagined Danka's mother Ytel, who must have stepped back, her instincts guiding her heart. She surely knew what the soldier was capable of doing to Danka; yet, she must have stepped back in hopes that her daughter could survive. Danka, at that moment — running for her life — could have no idea where the German soldiers were taking her mother.

Marian's silence seemed overwhelming. We had touched on the most painful of memories. He had managed to make an incisive cut into the images flashing through his mind, separating what he could put into words and piling the rest into a hole he could quickly bury again, keeping some things from my sight, perhaps protecting us both.

I couldn't help thinking back to what Marian had told me, months before, as we sat in my kitchen: that his own mother Rivka and brother Menache had also been taken in September of 1942. It appeared now that I had stumbled upon the context in which Marian's mother and twin had been arrested. I still didn't understand the exact circumstance of their deaths, but Marian's reaction suggested now that he was reliving the nightmare he had sought to avoid on the boat with Eliane. Had I asked too much of him? My mind wished comfort for him. Perhaps the telling would help.

"So Danka told her own children little stories," Marian said, breaking the silence with a nod to Danka, the woman who had created a fissure in his tightly packed and well-hidden nightmare. He was speaking of the time well after his own escape.

"Danka used to love to tell stories. I remember listening to her tales when we were in hiding together. We weren't always together. At one point after we left the Ghetto, Elsa and Danka were staying together. I was with Joseph, in one place; Elsa, Danka, and her father Jacob were in another place. That was during and after the Polish Uprising in 1944," Marian added, with no sign that he wanted to go on with his own story. Danka's stories could delight and distract a child yet wrench the heart from an old man's chest.

Marian was spent and I was emotionally exhausted. Ella, however, was full of energy and running through the house with LJ close behind. Conversations were ending in the next room. It was time for us to stop.

I left the room, with Marian now happily engrossed again by the ongoing birthday celebration. I prayed that I hadn't gone too far, and was mid-prayer when Carol took me aside.

"I don't remember, in the all the years we have been married, I don't remember him ever talking so much about what happened. I hope this helps him," she said, voicing my own thoughts. I hadn't realized Carol was in the kitchen, listening to Marian's storytelling. Her words were a comfort to me.

Marian's memory of Danka's storytellings reminded me of a story Bobby once told me. He has warm happy memories of childhood visits with his aunt, and one scenario still brings a smile to his face and a little laugh to his recounting. Danka loved to tell him stories too. He remembers sitting at her side, a young boy enthralled with the story de jour.

"She would finish the story and I didn't want it to stop," he said. "I would look up at her and say, '*et alors?*' She would laugh and continue. She was always able to add a little bit more."

Our eightieth birthday with Marian ended in emotional and loving goodbyes. It was time for time off, for mulling all we had heard, for letting things be. But it would not be for long.

Two months after his birthday celebration, Marian came to stay overnight before heading to the city for an early morning business meeting. I had more questions to ask, but did not plan an interview; I didn't want our visits to be only about "our project."

Sometime earlier I had asked Marian to bring the photographs he had shown me at his birthday celebration, and I would restore the damaged images and make digital copies. Bobby hadn't seen the pictures that day at Marian's house. Thus before dinner, the two of them pored over the faces Bobby was seeing for the first time.

At my kitchen table over dinner, the conversation had a casual spin — current events and economic trends. Somewhere in the middle of our leisurely dinner, however, and without so much as a prompt, Marian turned to his experiences before and during his stay in the Ghetto, in the months before the fateful September day.

The bits and pieces of meaning flowed without hesitation. Fearing I would distract Marian if I left the table to fetch my recorder, I grabbed a notepad within my reach and began the task of documenting these new stories. At this point Marian could simply pluck out significant morsels of memory that now lay close to the surface. One was the story he had so carefully covered with debris from his wartime experiences, in an attempt to stop the endless recreations and "what-ifs." It was an extraordinary story:

"The day my mother and my brother Menache were taken, just a few days before Danka and her own mother had been selected — at the beginning of September 1942 — I was working at Toebbens's and heard the sounds of another *Aktion* — another dreaded rounding-up of Jews. I was afraid I would be arrested if they found me, 'kay? I knew of a space to hide — a space above the file cabinets in the ceiling of the doctor's office where Elsa worked. I climbed onto the cabinets and into the space in the ceiling, concealing my hiding space with the ceiling boards. I stayed in the tiny space for the rest of the day. Showing myself would have cost me my life.

"Even Elsa didn't know where I was. I crawled out of the double ceiling late that night, only to learn from her that my mother and brother had been selected," Marian said. His voice conveyed the relief of finally sharing this scene. Thinking Menache would be safer staying with her in Toebbens's office, Rivka must have brought him to work with her on that particular day. Had Marian not hidden, the police would have taken him too: this, then, is the thought that still haunts him a lifetime later. The "what-if" of a terrible day long ago.

A wise woman once told me that I took too much credit for the negative, painful things in my life. Now I could see that agony in Marian's face. Perhaps he blamed himself for saving his own life and not protecting his mother and brother. I can imagine Elzbieta and even her father Israel feeling so too. It has taken Marian a good part of his life to accept the fact that luck — in the form of a German Jew who remembered his adorable face — his own resourcefulness, and the life-risking kindnesses of others had made all the difference in his world.

My own researches helped me now. In Michal Grynberg's volume of eyewitness accounts of what had transpired in the Warsaw Ghetto, I found corroborating descriptions of the selections that began in that summer of 1942. The construction of the death camp at Treblinka, the round-ups by haughty German soldiers, the Jewish factory workers safe at first and then sent to camps, the Ghetto population reduced by

310,000 through four months of deportations in summer-fall 1942 —
what I unearthed about my husband's family was appalling. I wanted to
hold Marian in my arms, for all that had befallen him.

So much was coming together: Rivka and Menache's arrest; Ytel's
selection and deportation; Marian's release from the selection site, along
with Elzbieta, Joseph, and Jacob; and the decision to find help on the
outside. Elzbieta knew there was no choice but to risk escaping to the
Aryan side.

Eliane had told me how Elzbieta lived outside the Ghetto with
Danka for a short time — the two beautiful Jewish women living in the
city, passing as Catholic Poles. Elzbieta had bleached Danka's hair a
soft, golden blond and secured papers to keep them both safe, but
there were so many dangers — both anticipated and unpredictable. So
many risks needing layers of safety. So many horrible ways to survive.

Praga, Warsaw, 1943

*Elzbieta knew she had to be careful and discreet; the
safe house she and Danka shared did not have a functioning
bathroom and they needed to dispose of their excrement
without causing suspicion. Elzbieta had an idea: they would
carry away their feces in a shopping bag, looking for a safe
and sanitary way to dispose of it. It was an unpleasant task
but, unlike their earlier work experiences, a job that brought
them to laughter.*

*With their false baptismal certificates, Elzbieta and
Danka were able to secure new work together in a clinic.*

Danka posed as a nurse, with Elzbieta at her side protecting her and guiding her through the care of their patients. They were usually together when the Nazis came into the hospital, determined to find "hidden" Jews and other enemies of the state with their horrific games. Elzbieta had prepared Danka for the inevitable — the constant tests the Germans obviously enjoyed — tests of hidden emotions and identities.

Sometimes their games were simple: the soldiers would shoot babies and see who reacted — suffering in some noticeable way — as if caring were a challenge to Nazi authority. Even a caring born of humanity could prove fatal. Elzbieta worked hard to teach Danka how to act as if she were indifferent. When the Gestapo tried to take away a teenage girl and her mother stood in front of her child to protect her, the young nurses continued their work as the Nazis put a bayonet through both of them — through the mother and, with enough length to the blade to be effective, through the daughter.

One afternoon brought a more direct encounter, one that would drive home how close they were to the death that danced around them daily.

Elzbieta and Danka had just left the clinic when they heard the sound of boots striking the pavement behind them. Casually looking over her shoulder, Elzbieta assessed the two soldiers who returned her gaze. The two men stopped them and the girls instinctively reacted to the two young men who looked them over with mischief in their eyes: Elzbieta and Danka began to flirt. They sat talking, the girls with their legs crossed, the two men eying their stockinged calves and ankles.

Elzbieta noticed the soldier's sudden, halted gaze and his smile morphing into a nauseating grin. One of the men had noticed something, something about their shoes. Could it have been mud or sawdust? Something that placed them in a questionable area, perhaps a farm outside the city? In an insightful flash, Elzbieta realized it was the new shoes she had acquired from a friend in the Ghetto workshop. He had made new shoes for the two of them as well as for Marian, Joseph, and his father. Elzbieta had heard the women in the clinic talking about the shoes, but she hadn't realized how precious they were until this moment.

The men began to grill the girls about their shoes, questioning them about the "friend" who had somehow found just the right size shoes. Elzbieta and Danka managed to change the subject with their smiles, their flirtatious giggles, and a suggestion that they go for a date. The two beautiful and resourceful women were able to win the men over, convincing them that they would rendezvous in a few hours, after going home to freshen up. Elzbieta and Danka must have giggled and coyly looked back over their shoulders as they walked away — walked away from death.

There were kinds as well as degrees of safety. Elzbieta knew that theirs were ever changing. Both had learned this lesson all too painfully, in the recent months, within the Ghetto.

The *Aktions* of 1942

The construction of a death camp at Treblinka was completed in the summer of 1942. In July, the Latvian and Ukrainian auxiliaries, along with the Jewish Security Police, began to help the Germans cordon off the Ghetto, section by section, conducting selections for deportation. With the Germans directing the choice of Jews for "resettlement," the security forces went through the streets, summoning inhabitants outside, and warning the hiding Jews that anyone who stayed behind would be shot. Marian, much like the other witnesses whose testimonies I would read, described how clean-shaven German soldiers, clad in their shining boots and finely tailored uniforms with belts — masterfully tanned and dressed bands of leather, meticulously locked in place around their waists — were assisted by uniformed, but beltless, Ukrainian auxiliaries when they fired their weapons to frighten the Jews.

Terrified residents rushed to the streets to show the soldiers the papers proving that German factories, workshops, or hospitals employed them. Good papers didn't always help; many Jews with documented proof that they worked in German-owned factories were sent to the left — to the death side of the selection, for no apparent reason. The soldiers would check each apartment to make sure it was empty, and chase those residents who were too slow, resistant, or discovered in their hiding spaces, oftentimes killing them on the spot.

During the day, while workers were at their jobs, the Germans would enter factory apartments and remove families as well as any workers from the night shift, taking these frightened people to the gathering place, the site known as *Umschlagplatz*, before shipping them via freight trains to Treblinka. Hundreds of thousands of people were sent to the death camps or killed within the Ghetto walls during these summer deportations.

During the first phase in the summer of 1942, hospital staff and workers employed by German companies were exempt from "resettlement" orders; Ghetto residents who could prove they were productively employed were allowed to stay, and some excused workers were quartered at their job sites, suggesting they were exempt from deportation. By late August, Toebbens's and Schultz's shops were among the handful of factories still providing seemingly safe havens for Ghetto residents. When the Germans left to liquidate other Jewish centers in the provinces, the Jewish police, who did not have guns or official uniforms, often wearing just an identifying armband and a badge, exclusively carried out the *Aktions* inside the Ghetto. Each police officer was ordered to round up a quota of people within a few hours and, upon presenting them at *Umschlagplatz*, was given a receipt that he turned in at the police headquarters. This receipt provided the necessary documentation that a quota was satisfied and then, only then, was he able to secure a meager portion of the heavily rationed food.

As the summer deportations progressed, even the highly valued documents held by workers at Toebbens's and Schultz's factories were useless, and the roundups reached into the factories. Pulling workers from shops at random, the Germans made capricious decisions as to whom they would select: every tenth person, young workers, children, older workers, or women. The Germans, or their representatives,

continued

The *Aktions* of 1942 continued

occasionally asked the Jews gathered for selection for their profession in
the Ghetto — arbitrarily determining whether a detainee's employment
was essential; other times they simply looked at a person's face and made
their critical decision — pointing to the left or right, to death or freedom.

In September 1942, the Ghetto's population was reduced to one-
tenth its original size; approximately 310,000 Jews were transported in
freight trains from the Warsaw Ghetto to Treblinka from July 22 to
October 3, 1942. The dilemma faced by the remaining Jews was
whether they should stay, or risk escaping to the Aryan side of the
walls. On the other side, they needed money and friends; one false
step, one nosey neighbor, one too many casual conversations with a
Pole could ruin plans, or worse, endanger your own life as well as anyone associated with you. Staying meant certain death.

7

The Comfort of Poetry, 1943-44

"If I had been asked in my early youth whether I preferred
to have dealings only with men or only with books, my answer would
certainly have been in favor of books. In later years this has become
less and less the case. Not that I have had so much better
experiences with men than with books; on the contrary, purely delightful
books even now come my way more often than purely
delightful men. But the many bad experiences with men have nourished
the meadow of my life as the noblest book could not do,
and the good experiences have made the earth into a garden for me."

– Martin Buber

After his escape from the Ghetto, Marian spent a good deal of his time on the Aryan side with the Rozenfarbs —Joseph, Danka, and their father Jacob. Hoping to learn more about Marian's time with my husband's father Joseph and his family, I asked Marian how they had passed the days in the attic in Praga. "What did you do when you were in hiding?" I asked. "What did you talk about during the years you spent in hiding?" I amended, before he could respond to my first inquiry.

"I pretty much stayed to myself and didn't talk much, 'kay?" he confessed, with a look of someone trying hard to tease an image out of long-suppressed memory. Then Marian suddenly smiled, and answered my first question: "Danka made me a beautiful jacket to wear." He smoothed his hands along his torso, as if showing off her fine sewing skills. "She sewed it for me *by hand!*" he added with pride, emphasizing Danka's accomplishment. I had known Danka was an artist — a painter — but I had not known, until this conversation with Marian, that Danka was a fashion designer, that she worked in London after the war, commanding an impressive salary for her designs.

"I couldn't wear the beautiful boots Elsa had given me. I remember a man at Toebbens named Perlman, Yitzhak Perlman, made them for me," he said, laughing at this memory and the coincidence of the name. "Elsa had Perlman make me my high boots. The high boots were quite the fashion then. I remember how beautiful they were. When I left the Ghetto, she made me promise I would never wear the boots outside, 'kay? They would attract attention. No one had brand new boots unless they got them from the workshops!"

I understood, in this moment, why the Nazi soldiers had noticed something strange about Elzbieta's shoes that day — the day Elzbieta and Danka had escaped by flirting with the enemy.

"I loved those boots. So, I wore my boots and jacket in the attic!" Marian said, with obvious delight at the image of himself wearing his finery out of sight of the world.

"Danka also made a sketch of Elsa, 'kay? It was a remarkable likeness." Marian's expression showed his sadness, remembering the loss of Danka's extraordinary artwork, a casualty of the war.

"Marian, what did you talk about? In all the time you spent in the attic, what did you talk about?" I asked him, pressing, in hopes of learning more about the Rozenfarbs.

"I read, read, and read all the time we were in hiding," he responded, distracted by these unshared memories.

"What did you read? What kept your attention during those years?"

"I read Mickiewicz. A book of poetry, an epic poem called *Pan Tadeusz*," he replied with a smile. Marian's gaze shifted to another place and time as he began reciting passages from Adam Mickiewicz's poem:

Litwo! Ojczyzno moja! Ty jeste jak zdrowie; . . .

I could not understand a word of the Polish pouring from Marian's heart and into my ears. I could understand what the memory of the passages meant to Marian — how the nostalgic sounds of the Polish language and the imagery of the romantic love poem had embraced him against the horrors of the war.

"It is a poem about the love of country, 'kay?" Marian explained, noting my puzzled look. "It celebrates everyday life — the day-to-day of the characters in Lithuania in the early 1800s. Mickiewicz wrote it while he was in exile in Paris — as were many other Polish intellectuals, in the 1830s."

Pan Tadeusz, which had become the national poem of Poland before the century of Marian's birth, is described as having the elements of a romantic historical novel: a feud between two families, a love story crossed by the feud, and a mysterious figure who dominates the action. Creating an idealized picture of life for succeeding generations, the narrative embodies the sentiments and idyllic way of life of the Polish gentry.

Clearly, I now sensed, Marian was not eager to talk further of the time spent with the Rozenfarbs. I did not press him.

I would learn, some months later, how Elzbieta had rescued him from the attic for a few months. She had rented a room from a Polish woman who had a large apartment on Jerusalem Avenue.

"The Polish woman must have known we were Jewish," Marian reflected. "But she never questioned Elsa or the 'legal' papers we had secured. We were there for several months. Elsa went to work during the day and I stayed in the apartment most of the time. The apartment was on the third floor and had two entrances. Before long the woman rented another room to someone else, someone we didn't know.

"I was home with Elsa one day, shortly after the new tenant moved in, 'kay? We heard a knock on the apartment door. It was strange to have someone knock on the door, so I asked the Polish woman to ask who was there. We heard the sound of the men's voices and realized they were the Gestapo. When the woman did not respond, they shouted for her to open the door. I grabbed Elsa by the arm, took whatever clothing was nearby, and pushed her ahead of me to the service entrance. I remember the winding staircase to the ground floor, the sound of the Gestapo shouting, and the light from their flashlights hitting the walls of the stairwells above us. When we reached street level I peeked out the door. Two Gestapo agents stood by an archway at the building entrance. We couldn't leave!

"Elsa and I ran back inside and up another flight of stairs to the roof. I was hoping we could jump to the roof of the next building. The roof was too steep, 'kay? We couldn't even go out and stand on it and the next roof was too far below us. I remember looking out on our roof and noticing snowflakes; it was a cold, snowy December day and we didn't have coats. When we first ran from the apartment I grabbed a shirt for myself. The only thing I could find for Elsa was a bathrobe — a green bathrobe.

"We ran down the stairs again and I saw the agents still waiting outside, so we exited the stairwell and entered the dimly lit hallways of the apartment house. We began making our way to the other side of the building, 'kay? Down a hallway, I saw a woman coming out of an apartment with a bundle of trash. I grabbed Elsa's arm and we walked down the hall toward the woman's apartment. I put my foot in the doorway as the woman walked back inside and tried to close the door behind her. I noticed that the apartment was a doctor's office — his name was on the door. I smiled at her and said, 'We are here to see the doctor.' She knew exactly what we were doing. Everyone could hear the Gestapo yelling throughout the building as they continued searching for us. She nodded and told us to stay in the waiting room while she got the doctor."

Marian was speaking more spontaneously with each of our conversations. Listening to him tell his story now with such clarity and youthful enthusiasm, I imagined the doctor hearing the commotion and emerging from his examination room, careful not to alarm the patient sitting quietly within the room's protective sterility. Assessing Marian and Elzbieta, and their obvious desperation, he must have looked into their eyes and recognized their humanity as well as his own.

"He told us quietly that we could stay in the waiting room. He said that if anyone came in and asked, he would vouch for us — tell them we were his patients. I remember sitting there, in the waiting room, when the doctor's young son came in and asked me if I wanted to play chess with him. They saved us from the Gestapo. The other tenant in our apartment, the new one, wasn't so lucky."

Marian was quiet again for the long moment it took him to dwell on this experience. I envisioned the doctor's son who, through the kindness he offered Marian, became another nameless rescuer. Marian had retrieved cherished memories of his rescuers and, along with their images, the gratitude he had felt. With a simple game of chess, his young rescuer had lent moments of normalcy to a day suffused in terror.

"We waited for a bit," Marian now continued. And then went out into the street. I remember hailing a horse and buggy. Elsa asked me what I was doing. We had no money and didn't know where we were going to go. 'Look at you,' I said. Elsa looked down at herself. She was standing in the snow-covered street wrapped in a green bathrobe. We had no choice but to get into the buggy and go somewhere nearby, 'kay? Anywhere safe.

"We were lucky. Elsa had friends a short distance away who paid for the buggy ride and kept us for the night. I remember that it was December 2, 1943 — the nearest we ever came to being caught. And you wonder why Elsa and I were so close?" Marian whispered, looking up at me over the rim of his glasses. I was understanding so much now.

"Was this even nearer than the time with Stasio?" I asked after some silence, reacting to his assessment of the danger with Elzbieta, and aware of their bond.

"Maybe. But they didn't want me. The Gestapo wanted Stasio. They took me because I was there."

I knew Elzbieta had experienced a narrow escape from the Gestapo. She had told Bobby that on one occasion she was so frightened she almost swallowed the cyanide pill. Perhaps this was that time— the time she believed the Nazis would arrest them, and deport them to separate places.

Marian would return to Praga and the attic for several more months. He and Joseph then left the safety of Praga in July of 1944; the confining attic had finally become unbearable. Two more days in Praga and they would have been liberated by the Russians, but it was not to be so. Instead, they hid in the basement of an apartment building in Warsaw proper during the Polish Uprising. I had known of Marian and Joseph's hiding in an apartment building during this second horrific uprising, which began on August 1, 1944. Yet I had not known that they sat huddled in the cold basement of a building across the street from German barracks, listening to Germans killing Poles on the other side of the basement walls.

Elzbieta had arranged yet another safe place. Her contact Stanislaw Kudelski worked as superintendent for an apartment house in Mokotow, just south of Warsaw proper. Marian and Joseph stayed in the apartment house basement while she hid with Danka and Jacob somewhere in the middle of the city. The apartment house was a stone's throw away from the soldiers' quarters, making it a less obvious place for Jews to hide.

"Kudelski provided a one-room apartment in the building in which he worked on Kazimierzowska Street," Marian told me. "In the first days of the Uprising, the Germans ordered everyone to leave the building. Joseph was afraid of being identified as a Jew because of his Semitic features, so he hid in the double ceiling of the apartment. A German officer watched me as I left the apartment, closing the door behind me. I was told to stand outside with the other tenants, and when I was allowed to return to the apartment, I found Joseph safe in his hiding place. We were lucky this time but we sought a safer place to hide in the days to come.

"There was a removable section of a wall in the basement, behind which you could access the water pipes and the dirt ground under the building. We dug a hole in the dirt, just large enough for Joseph to fit inside. There was no light for him to see what was around him, 'kay? It was my job to find food and water for the two of us."

Marian, with his life-saving looks and the papers secured through Stasio's contact, could pass as a non-Jewish Pole — risking excursions through the streets of Warsaw looking for food. Joseph, whose dark complexion and brown eyes made him more suspect, did not have the same choices. Thus after leaving the confining space of an attic in Praga, where they had spent over a year, Marian and Joseph now had to hide in the basement of the apartment building for nine frightening weeks.

"We knew the killing was going on all around us, and spent weeks in this hiding place, waiting for the Russians to enter the city and liberate us." Then Marian began telling me about the Polish Uprising, soon to rage in the streets nearby.

The Uprising, the Polish Home Army's attempt to liberate Warsaw from Nazi occupation, began on August 1, 1944. The Polish army expected to fight for a few days until the Soviet Army reached the city. The Soviet advance stopped short of the city, however, and instead of fighting the Germans alongside the Poles, they observed the fighting from the other side of the Vistula River. Historians state that the Russians and Poles had so much fighting between them that the Russians relished the defeat of the Polish army: they watched as the Polish resistance fought German occupation until the Polish Home Army surrendered. This fact would deeply affect our family's lives.

"I could hear the sounds of gunfire in the streets of Warsaw outside the basement walls," Marian recalled. "And the orders from a German soldier to shoot — to shoot Poles who were just one hundred yards away. The second day of the uprising, I went outside only to encounter a German soldier. A quick look of acknowledgement passed between us as I tried to place his familiar face. The boy in the German uniform was a Jew, 'kay?, someone I had recently met; his name was Andre. Kudelski had introduced us to Andre shortly after Joseph and I arrived in Warsaw. We were all in Kudelski's apartment and Kudelski told me that I had something in common with Andre, the young man then dressed in civilian clothes. Kudelski probably helped countless other Jews during the war.

"Andre, now wearing an SS uniform, recognized me. With shame distorting his face he came over to me and spoke in a hoarse, restrained voice. 'I had to do it. I had to save my life,' he said, confessing his betrayal. He had faked his genealogy and was passing as a German citizen and working as a conductor on a streetcar when the fighting began. Andre chose to join the German army, while Kudelski fought alongside the other Polish patriots.

"Andre asked me what I needed and I told him food, a loaf of bread. He brought me food whenever he could, and then he disappeared, right before the liberation. He had told me it was not safe, for either of us, to be seen together. He may have been afraid I would betray him. I never found out what happened to him, 'kay?, but I suspect that the Germans never really trusted him — Andre never carried a gun and perhaps that is why." I heard no judgment in Marian's voice. People did what they had to do to survive, and Andre had dared to help them.

"While we were in hiding, Joseph asked me to find him a glass container so he could hide his gold and Russian coins in the basement floor. These valuables had secured our safety with Stasio's cousins as well as with Kudelski. Later, once it was safe to retrieve the glass container, Joseph was unable to find it. It was not where he remembered hiding it — the location he had shown me. Because only I knew where he had buried the gold, Joseph accused me of stealing it. I was so angry and hurt. The two of us fought," Marian recalled, still suffering and visibly agitated after all these years.

"Joseph repeated his accusation to Elsa, 'kay? She spoke to me and I showed her the location I remembered, the spot Joseph had shown where he had buried the gold. When she and I dug further into the ground we found the gold and the coins. Joseph and I had been through so much together, and yet he was able to think I was untrustworthy," Marian said, still in anguish more than fifty years beyond that day. In Joseph's defense, Marian revealed, the bunker experience changed Joseph, made him anxious and suspicious for a time. How could it not have? How could anyone not be changed forever by the Warsaw atrocities?

Marian noted that Joseph's accusation fractured their relationship, and he never fully forgave Joseph for not trusting him. It was not clear whether Joseph had ever apologized. Theirs was a quiet undercurrent, however, and our families may have found it difficult to mend.

I learned from Marian that Kudelski's apartment building was evacuated in late 1944, but he was given permission to stay. With the end of the war in March 1945, Marian, Elzbieta, Joseph, Jacob, and a number of their friends — including Leon Kriger — all lived there, in the apartments on Kazimierzowska Street.

I had always assumed that Marian had gotten to know Bobby's father Joseph better than anyone who knew him. They had spent so much time together, their lives changing irrevocably with shared experiences. Yet when I pressed him for information about Joseph, Marian spoke only of his life both immediately before and immediately after the war. It was clear that Marian felt a need — a responsibility — to hold his tongue.

He did tell me that as a boy Joseph Rozenfarb had lived with his parents and siblings in an apartment house in an affluent neighborhood in Zoliborz, north of Warsaw proper. Joseph's father Jacob had built the house and still owned it in 1939, when the Germans forced them to leave. Joseph took Marian to see the apartment house after the war and to Marian's amazement it had survived the Nazi's demolition spree.

"We were able to enter the house with one of Joseph's big brawny friends standing watch for the current owners," Marian would tell me in the months to come.

"Someone had discovered the hiding place in the attic—the double wall Jacob had created to store the valuables they had to leave behind, 'kay? There was a huge hole in the wall and very little of value left behind it for us to retrieve. We were able to grab some silver Jacob had hidden in the attic and a portrait Danka had painted of Joseph. We got out of there as quickly as we could," Marian would tell me, the muscles in his body tensing as he relived helping Joseph "steal" what was left of the Rozenfarbs' possessions.

Today Bobby and I have Danka's large portrait of Joseph, pipe in hand and seeming almost regal as he looks out over his left shoulder, confronting the viewer. I put the oil painting in storage when Bobby brought it home after Joseph died. At that time, the bullet holes the Nazis left as a reminder of their visit to the Rozenfarb home were not the kind of artifact I cared to display. That was then. Now the painting hangs in my studio, undergoing necessary restoration.

I had known that Joseph lost his younger brother Stanislaw before the war. Stanislaw died of leukemia in his late teens, and it was Joseph's need to commemorate the short life of the brother he adored that inspired him to change his family name to Rostan— "Ro" from Rozenfarb and "stan" from Stanislaw.

Joseph, his older brother Leon, and their friend Mark Labendz —Danka's future husband—had been soldiers in the Polish cavalry. Joseph would puff out his chest when he described the cavalry to Marian, and would one day do the same as he told his son about this elite branch of the Polish army. His descriptions were vivid.

"The soldiers wore elegant boots and the finest tailored uniforms. They were fantastic," he told Bobby, his only child. "We came from the finest homes—the landowners and well-educated intelligentsia." This was as far as Joseph would go in his stories about the war and his life before. Marian must have heard Joseph's stories of the cavalry many times, perhaps too many times, as they spent endless hours, days, and months hiding together. He must have told Marian how the cavalrymen fought German tanks in the fall of 1939—by luring them into rough terrain and attacking with anti-tank guns, horse artillery, and anti-tank ammunition. Joseph probably described the cavalry's first encounter with Hitler's vaunted *Wehrmacht*: a tactical success, at negligible cost. He may not have dwelled on the fact that this victory was short-lived; before the Poles could reorganize, a column of German tanks and motorized troops arrived, unleashing a devastating hail of fire. The Poles suffered terrible losses before they turned their horses and retreated, abandoning a recently won field to the advancing Germans.

Eliane would tell me how Joseph, returning from the fight alone, without Leon, approached his family's apartment house only to have his mother Ytel chase him away. He was so unrecognizable, in his filth and weariness, that Ytel thought he was a dangerous stranger. The family dog, using his keen sense of smell, was the first to recognize his beloved master and run to him, tail wagging and tongue eagerly cleansing Joseph's tired and dirty face. Leon returned home soon afterwards, eager to retrieve his wife Hanna, and their teenage son Zdzislaw, whom they called "Zjeeshu." Their reunion was short-lived. The Germans soon came for Leon and his family, and they became the Rozenfarb family's first casualties of the war.

I first learned the location of Joseph's home that night in May 2010, when Marian came for his brief visit and described his escape from the *Aktion* by hiding in the ceiling of Elzbieta's infirmary. That same night,

I showed Marian a map I had found depicting Warsaw before the war. Marian was moved to joyous tears when I shared the map—a drawing I had found on the Internet that allowed me to see where all his stories had taken place. I never expected such a deeply pleased response, and I welcomed it.

Elated by the image of his lost city, Marian pointed to the site of Benjamin's gravel transport business, an office on Jerusalem Avenue not far from Elzbieta's Dentorex office. He showed me where he lived with his family before the war, in an apartment just north of the area marked "Srodmiescie," near the center of the city. He also found the apartment house in Mokotow, at 85 Kazimierzowska Street, apartment 11, where he and Joseph stayed during the Polish Uprising and after the war.

That same night, as Marian sat at my kitchen table showing me memorable sites on the map, he traced, with his finger, his escape route to Praga—the one he had taken via trolley car and a run through the back streets, when the Gestapo arrested Stasio.

Praga, Warsaw, 1943

"O Lithuania, my country, thou
Art like good health; I never knew till now
How precious, till I lost thee. Now I see
Thy beauty whole, because I yearn for thee."

Elzbieta heard the lines of poetry echo in her dream as
she tried to envision Marian hiding then in the attic in
Praga—hoping to comfort herself and allay her own fears.

It didn't take much effort to imagine him, almost reach out and touch him, as he read the opening lines of Pan Tadeusz, *once again, and closed his eyes before sleep. Elzbieta knew that Marian's ritual was the key to a few hours of peaceful dreams — dreams of his childhood, of his life before. The soporific effect of reciting the poetry lines was of great comfort, when memories and fear of the world outside brought Marian to his knees.*

In the hidden attic in Praga, Marian sat leaning against a wall, trying to keep his face against the cool, numbing plaster. Joseph and Jacob kept their voices low as they argued over some transaction that had occurred years ago. Marian had no idea what they were talking about. He wanted so desperately not to have to hear their hoarse voices as they tried to argue without making too much noise.

The goat was resting nearby, chewing on something Marian could no longer recognize. He was too tired to get up and check what it was, what their four-legged roommate had stolen. It was a good idea to keep the goat up here, he thought to himself. The animal's restlessness made a good excuse for the noise drifting down to the apartment below. Stasio must have thought of it, he mused.

Marian looked over at Danka, sitting with some material in her lap as she carefully examined the stitches she had just completed. Marian envied Danka's talent for making things — doing something productive as they sat day after day, waiting for the world to come back to them. She had cut his hair just yesterday, and he brushed the bangs back from his forehead as the memory came to mind. Danka smiled at him and his face must have turned red, because he could feel the warmth of a blush in his cheeks. He knew she watched over him and gave reports to Elzbieta. He didn't want his sister to worry about him; she had enough to think about just keeping herself alive, let alone the people who depended upon her hyper-vigilance. Marian smiled back and lifted the book, *Pan Tadeusz*, to show her that he was reading. Danka nodded and looked back upon the jacket she had fashioned for Marian out of a discarded coat.

I will need the warmth of the jacket when we get out of here, he thought. Maybe Danka knows something. . . . He dismissed the thought as soon as he felt it overtaking him, and turned to the dog-eared pages of his book.

Marian closed his eyes and, in a soft whisper, repeated the lines of Mickiewicz's epic poem as if he were standing in front of his class, on a bright, sunny day:

> "Thus fate ends all things with a clapper stroke.
> The mind's profoundest thoughts and fancy's flights,
> The joys of friendship, innocent delights,
> The heart's outpourings — at the brazen roar
> All's broken and confused and is no more."

In a farmhouse too many miles away, Elzbieta slept fitfully as she imagined Marian facing some vague, indecipherable danger even with the end of the war.

8

The Aftermath, 1945-50

"I am in fact a quarter Jewish, and though I did not
"hate" the idea of being taken for a Jew,
I did not precisely like it, particularly under these circumstances.
I wished it to be clear that I had left the club car for
intellectual and principled reasons;
I wanted those men to know that it was not I,
but my principles, that had been offended.
To let them conjecture that I had left because I was Jewish
would imply that only a Jew could
be affronted by an anti-Semitic outburst; a terrible idea."

– Mary McCarthy

Even after the war ended, Elzbieta was not convinced that as Jews, they were safe from further harm. She continued using the Polish surname Rajewska after the war, as would Joseph Rozenfarb and his father Jacob. Elzbieta's concerns were well founded: waves of anti-Jewish assaults and pogroms took place all across Poland, from mid-1944 to the summer of 1946, when more than 100,000 Polish Jews left their nation. Elzbieta was particularly worried for Marian's safety and well-being after the war. She must have understood his enduring more loss and suffering than most children are equipped to handle; she sought out a safe and healthy environment for her young brother in 1945 — a home and school for orphans — just outside of Warsaw. Marian was fifteen. He referred to the school now as a "home for surviving youth."

It was a memorable time for Marian. With excitement and an air of privilege, he told me about the numerous university professors and professionals—the dedicated, intelligent, and compassionate faculty—who now gathered with one goal in mind. Their goal: to provide the youngest survivors, the children and young adolescents, with a rich education—teaching them what they needed to know to get back on track with their lives.

"We had small groups of students studying math and science with our instructors. We were able to catch up in a few months, 'kay?" Marian spoke with an almost youthful pride in his academic accomplishments.

I would learn about Zatrzebie, the home for orphans of the war, after reading Lucjan Dobroszycki's book, *Survivors of the Holocaust in Poland: A Portrait Based on Jewish Community Records, 1944-1947*. One particular paragraph caught my attention: the comparison of the number of Jewish children before and after the war. On the eve of World War II, there were close to a million Jewish children, age fourteen or younger, in Poland. Documents suggest that throughout Poland, somewhere around five thousand Jewish children survived the war—in Dobroszycki's words: "only a handful." I did not fully appreciate the implication of this small number until I scanned the lists Dobroszycki included—lists of Jewish children who survived. There, toward the end of the alphabetized list of children in orphanages and children's homes in December 1945, I found Marian's name. A typographical error referenced him as "Maria," but Marian was identifiable by virtue of his year of birth and his last known address: Zatrzebie. It was the first time I had seen the name of the home for children—a residence outside Warsaw—that Elzbieta had found for Marian.

The campus of Zatrzebie, I would learn from survivor Dov Visberg's memoir *I Remember*, was in a southeastern suburb of Warsaw. Marian had remembered the green grass and trees, but not the name of the "school." Before the war, the park-like campus surrounded by woods was a summer camp for children. In the summer of 1946, several wooden houses, each large enough to accommodate twenty to thirty children, were home to two hundred children — children from less than age three to those in their upper teens. Dov Visberg had attended the school along with Marian.

Zatrzebie, much like other postwar homes for Jewish children in Poland, was under the control of the Central Committee for Jews in Poland. The American Joint Jewish Committee helped with financial support and American Jews donated much-needed clothing. The children came from numerous places. Some emerged from hiding places among Polish Christians. A few were brought to the Central Committee by Poles who had protected them during the German occupation, their true identities sometimes unknown. Some came from concentration and extermination camps. Some came from families returning from wartime safety in the Soviet Union. All except the very youngest, who could not remember, told stories of their persecution and suffering and the many tricks, inventions, and near-miracles that helped them escape death. Some children had living parents, rarely both, but the parents were unable to support them. Zatrzebie took them all in.

Zatrzebie's instructors themselves came from various camps and hiding places; many were esteemed professional teachers with advanced academic degrees. The charge of the staff was to focus on psychological and educational rehabilitation. Most of the children had not attended school for years — likely the entire duration of the war — and the younger children had never been to school. Through intensive study and with the guidance of a dedicated faculty, the children worked hard to compensate for lost years.

With the help of her friends and contacts in the Central Committee, Elzbieta was able to find a more permanent safe haven for Marian, in England. Marian told me that a British rabbi, whom he remembered as Rabbi Schonfeld, arranged for him to go to school in London in March 1947.

I would learn that in the months leading up to the war in early 1938, Rabbi Solomon Schonfeld had created a rescue organization called the Chief Rabbi's Religious Emergency Council. The Council's purpose was to bring Orthodox rabbis and teachers to England — Jewish educators not sponsored by non-Jewish refugee organizations in Great Britain because they were considered "unproductive" citizens. With his faculty in place, Schonfeld now instituted a rabbinical academy and through the activities of the *kindertransport* he helped to create, Schonfeld brought two hundred and fifty refugee children to London from Vienna in the winter of 1938. Overall, Schonfeld procured entry permits for nearly 3,700 Jews who reached England before and right after the war.

Elzbieta took advantage of Schonfeld's academy project when the rabbi traveled to Poland after the war, seeking to bring war orphans to England. Schonfeld hired the Swedish boat the *Ragne* to transport the children to England, where the government allowed them to stay as long as they attended school. Qualifying for admission as a documented "orphan," Marian stayed in London for three years, until he was twenty. Dora, one of Israel's sisters, would sponsor his emigration to the United States and once he secured his visa, he left London for New York aboard the *Queen Elizabeth*.

I could never quite understand why Elzbieta sent Marian to England for schooling after the war. I had learned of the anti-Semitism in Poland after the war from Marian, who had thus far described only the overall discomfort and lack of security they felt living amongst the postwar Polish population of Warsaw. I would learn much more from Dov Visberg's and Lucjan Dobroszycki's accounts of life in Poland at that time, and the atmosphere of panic among Jewish society in the summer of 1946 when Jews, yet again, believed they could no longer be safe in Poland. Despite the large militia and army presence in the town of Kielce, in southeastern Poland, Jews were murdered there — on one occasion, in cold blood, in public, and for a horrific siege of more than five hours.

The acts of violence in Kielce commenced on July 4, 1946. The beatings and shootings followed a false tale of child kidnapping, allegations of blood libel, and ultimately a police investigation. A mob of local townsfolk, the police, and uniformed soldiers are said to have been responsible for the violence in which at least forty Jews died. With unanswered questions about the cause of the pogrom lingering for decades, an investigation in 1992 affirmed that the local authorities in Kielce failed to take decisive steps against the escalating post-war violence. Visberg's own account of the aftermath of the pogrom conveys the effects on the Jews in Warsaw and, particularly, the students at Zatrzebie:

"This put us on alert. Our feeling of security disappeared, and the importance of self-defense settled in our minds. In Zatrzebie all the older boys underwent a crash course in using rifles, and every night, two of us at a time, armed with rifles, patrolled the campus, changing with two others in the middle of the night. Fortunately, we never had to use the rifles, but our feeling of being 'at home' was badly shaken."

Dobroszycki notes that the Jewish population of postwar Poland would reach its peak in the summer of 1946, after the mass repatriation of Jews from the USSR; conservative estimates suggest the number as roughly 230,000. The Kielce pogrom initiated a precipitous decrease in the population of Polish Jews. Some 140,000 Jews left Poland in the eight months following mid-1946.

As we spoke so many years later in the spring of 2011, Marian was obviously still distressed by the memory of one incident in the rubble of postwar Warsaw:

"Two boys had been chasing me, calling me 'Jew' and worse, and threatening my life. I was running away from them — running through the deserted remains of buildings, 'kay? I was convinced I was in mortal danger — that they would harm me if they caught me. I picked up a brick and heaved it at one of the boys, not even taking aim. I just wanted to frighten them. I was horrified to see the brick hit one of the boys in his face and then blood pouring from the wound. I was sickened by the incident," Marian confessed. "I kept running, but I have never forgotten that day."

"It was not the first time I experienced fear from anti-Semitism after the war," he went on. "I had gone skiing at Zakopane with my classmates at Zatrzebie. Some boys started in with us there, but fortunately nothing came of it."

Ultimately, Marian and all surviving members of the Rozenblum and Rozenfarb families left postwar Poland for new lives elsewhere, fearing continued persecution, or worse.

Helping children remained an obsession for Elzbieta. Family lore has it that she was working as a nurse for a Jewish organization in Warsaw established to find the surviving families of children orphaned by the war. Records suggest that the organization was the Central Committee for Polish Jews and the school was Zatrzebie.

Elzbieta spent as much time as possible with Marian and the other young orphans, soothing those they could not reunite with family members and joyfully celebrating the fortunate ones who could return to familiar arms, if not homes. One little girl whose name appears on Dobroszycki's list of 1945 — a little girl who like Marian is identified as living at Zatrzebie — held Elzbieta's attention.

Jadzia knew her own name, but very little, if anything, about where she lived before her parents were taken from her. Elzbieta was more than eager to give little Jadzia the love and attention she craved. In return, the five-year-old child gave Elzbieta a sense of loving calm in the midst of a chaotic life. At that time and place in Warsaw right after

the war, Elzbieta and Joseph lived together using the Polish surname
Rajewska. The two began to spend more and more time with Jadzia.
I would eventually learn that Jadzia's parents had saved their six-month-
old child by giving her to a Christian woman — someone who worked
for them — just before their arrest in 1941. The woman hid Jadzia for
the duration of the war, and when the parents did not come to reclaim
her she placed Jadzia in an orphanage. Jadzia never saw the woman
again. The Central Committee for Jews in Poland, determined to find
a safe home for Jadzia, granted Elzbieta legal custody in 1947. The
little survivor had a new family, a new home, and a new name: Jadzia
Rajewska.

Elzbieta, Joseph, and Jadzia left Poland after the adoption and
began a new life in France. Elzbieta's father Israel and brother Adam
— both of whom had managed to find their way back to Warsaw and
Elzbieta after the war — joined them there, in the outskirts of Paris.
Marian was still in school in London, age seventeen in 1947.

The postwar Jewish community in Paris welcomed the family and
helped them begin building a new business. Israel secured credit from
local businessmen and, along with Adam and Elzbieta, had the skill
and experience needed to manufacture and sell men's clothing.

"My father had a talent for selling, 'kay?" Marian spoke enthusiastically. "He could sell anything! In France, he met with a man who man-
ufactured men's clothing and convinced the man to let him copy some
trouser patterns. Can you imagine?" Marian spoke with the pride of a
son boasting of his father's gifts. Elzbieta knew enough French to facilitate sales and was able to seek out storeowners and sell them the trousers.

They all lived and worked in an apartment in Neuilly, just outside
of Paris. During the day the apartment was a "factory," staffed with the
cutters, tailors, and pressers Israel hired to manufacture the trousers.
In the evening the apartment was home to Israel, Adam, Elzbieta,
Joseph, and little Jadzia.

Although the French government did allow Jews to stay in the country, it did not allow them to own a business. A French neighbor fronted their business venture — she was willing to help them and they paid her for the use of her name. The business slowly grew and Israel and Adam both remarried — Israel, I suspected, to his French business associate — a revelation that Marian let slip but was not too eager to acknowledge or discuss. Along with Adam and his new postwar family, Elzbieta, Joseph, and Jadzia settled into a stable and contented life in France.

The little girl thrived with her new family, convinced that life would be secure, loving, and predictable. Elzbieta and Joseph married, and with my husband Bobby's arrival in the spring of 1949, the family of four was flourishing and forward-looking. Almost sixty years later Jadzia, whom I know today as Yael — the name she would eventually choose for herself — would tell me of the unforgettable afternoon when Elzbieta eagerly arrived at the school to retrieve her, only to find she was not there. Hysterical with fear and demanding an explanation from the school's administrator, Elzbieta learned that Jadzia's "family" had come to the school to claim her.

Elzbieta had never been able to tell Bobby the whole story of Yael's abduction. For Bobby, Yael was the little girl his mother had cared for and who had stayed with them until they found her family. Until the moment in time, in the summer of 2009, when Yael sat with Bobby in our living room, weeping as she described what had happened, he had believed her departure to be amicable and anticipated. It was almost six decades after Yael left Elzbieta's safekeeping, when Bobby was sixty years old, that he learned of the kidnapping.

Yael, who by now was approaching age seventy, had come to the states with her husband Oded to reunite with Bobby before continuing on to visit their daughter and son-in-law in North Carolina. During her brief and emotional visit, Yael explained that her relatives had tracked her down through the Jewish agencies responsible for her after the war. Made aware of her adoption by Elzbieta, Yael's relatives had approached Elzbieta with their claim for her custody, or so she believed. With the confusion of a child whose parents let "strangers" take her away, Yael, sitting with us in our kitchen a lifetime later, tried to make sense of Elzbieta's actions long ago: both giving her up and then divorcing Joseph. "They always seemed so happy," she cried. "I never could understand why they gave me up and then divorced."

Marian would not venture deeply into this part of Elzbieta's life. He revealed only that Yael had been taken from Elzbieta — ostensibly kidnapped — and that his family got together and decided that it was best for the child not to try to fight Yael's family for custody.

Yael brought copies of some photographs for Bobby — photographs that Joseph had sent to her in 1960, as well as photographs of Elzbieta's visits to Israel when Yael was already married and had a family of her own. Three undated pictures Marian believed were taken in Paris, sometime in 1948, show a happy family — Elzbieta, Joseph, and Yael — with friends and family sharing their smiles and embraces. Elzbieta's loose-fitting blouse suggests that she was pregnant with Bobby when the pictures were taken. The note with all the photographs, "Montreal, 1960," suggests that this may have been the first time since her kidnapping that Joseph had made contact with Yael, who would have been nineteen by that time.

Another photograph was of Joseph holding two babies in his arms and a smiling Yael, a ribbon tied in a huge bow holding her hair in place, sitting next to them and leaning against Joseph's shoulder. The note at the bottom reads, "You, Robert, Eliane (my niece) and me. A short visit to Brussels, Belgium, in 1949, to show Robert and you to my family and friends. On this picture Robert has 5 months, and Eliane 7 months. Look how sweet and beautiful you are, my Yael." It is signed and dated from Montreal — July 1960. The picture, according to

Joseph, was taken in August of 1949, when Yael was eight years old. Elzbieta and Joseph had taken their two children to Brussels where Joseph's father Jacob and his sister Danka and her new husband Mark — Eliane's parents — had sought refuge and a fresh new beginning. Eliane had been born in Brussels, as was her younger sister Jacqueline, and Jacob died there in 1952, just a few years after the picture was taken.

Elzbieta always dated her separation from Joseph as sometime shortly after Bobby was born in March 1949. It's possible that Yael's kidnapping and Elzbieta's acquiescence to her family's demands caused the fissure that eventually divided the once-happy couple. One photograph Yael gave to Bobby speaks volumes. Unlike the other pictures of Bobby as an infant, this image was taken by a professional photographer in Paris. Seated and smiling for the photographer, the family bore no evidence of the not-so-distant past: Marian is dressed in a dark suit and looks healthy and vigorous; Israel, wearing a dark tie, jacket, and his new wedding ring, stares back at the photographer with a restrained smile; and Elzbieta, holding "Robert" in her lap, smiles kindly at the person documenting their survival. The family portrait is noteworthy for its absent members: Joseph and Yael. Yael and Joseph were no longer "in the picture" when my husband was approximately one year old.

In the spring of 2010, during her second visit to New York and shortly after her husband Oded's sudden death, Yael and her daughter Tsufit and three-month-old grandson Adam paid us another visit. This time, Yael would repeat her story for me.

We met at the Jewish Museum, on the Upper East Side of Manhattan, for an afternoon spent talking, eating, and discussing the museum's exhibitions. As we settled in for a quick lunch in the museum's café, I offered Yael two faded Polish documents I had placed in a protective plastic envelope. Bobby had already told Yael about the contents — the adoption papers Joseph had kept until he died and Bobby had subsequently stored, not realizing what the documents described. Yael was moved to tears, not only by the fact that the papers still existed, but also by the evidence that Elzbieta had been granted permission to adopt her. She had never understood what legal arrangements had been made for her when she left the orphanage. The fact that she had loved and trusted Elzbieta and Joseph had been enough at that moment in her life.

I had found the papers after Yael's first visit to New York, when I searched through a box of pictures that Joseph had saved. The faded cardboard tube, which Joseph had wrapped in brown paper, held four sheets of official documents, each typewritten in Polish.

During and after the war Joseph and his father Jacob had both used the same Polish surname that Elzbieta used: Rajewskiej or Rajewska. Two of the documents described Joseph and Jacob's surname change to Rostan, in 1947.

One of the other two documents, signed by the Central Committee for Jews in Poland in 1947 when Jadzia was six years old, gave "Elzy" Rutman-Rajewskiej custody of the little orphan. The other faded brown paper, also issued by the Central Committee — with the blue circular stamp of the Central Committee of Jews in Warsaw — stated that nothing was known about little "Jadwiga" beyond her name and the year of her birth, 1941.

Unrolling the two scrolls, Yael was visibly shaken; she pored over each word and tried to make sense of the typewritten Polish, a language that for her by now was undecipherable.

"Do you have a translation? In English?" she asked. I told her how Marian had recently translated the two documents into English, and described the information that each contained.

I was mesmerized by the whole idea of the existence of these worn, fragile papers, and by Yael's intense attention to documents with such immeasurable meaning for her. Yael, thinking much the way I was at that moment, asked me the very question I was pondering: "Why did

Joseph save these papers, bring them to Canada, and then store them so they would last — last long enough?" I shook my head, registering my incomprehension to both Yael and her daughter Tsufit. We all looked at the two scrolls, which insisted on rolling themselves up again once Yael, as best she could, had taken in the information.

"Can you imagine what happened?" she asked me, as I sat watching her smooth her hands over the old documents, as if touching them would grant her access to that moment in time when all was well.

I shook my head again, indicating that I could not imagine what any of them had gone through, while truthfully I was doing just that — imagining what Elzbieta and Joseph had gone through with the beloved presence and sudden absence of Yael.

"She is my mother, I told them at the school," Yael said, her voice quavering as she reached deep into her past, reliving her pain. Hers was the pain of losing a mother not once but twice; the pain of losing her childhood, a second time; the pain of losing her trust in adults who had "her best interest" at heart.

"It was my uncle who took me from the school," Yael now said. "One day he placed me in front of a mirror. He held a picture of my birth mother beside my face, so that I could see her face next to me. 'Look,' he said, raising his voice, 'look at your mother. That other woman is not your mother!' " Yael's voice trembled as she reenacted an encounter remembered all too clearly.

Yael stayed in the moment of her childhood and spoke of what she was reliving: "They came to my school and told me they were my family. I told them 'No, Elzbieta and Joseph are my family; I need to go to them.' They took me away from Elzbieta and I cried and cried, but they would not let me go to my home. I understood that my parents had died and that Elzbieta and Joseph were not my blood family, but I loved them, they were my life, my home.

"My uncle thought he was doing something good for me, but it was not good. It was not right," Yael said, as if analyses of the situation through the years had always led her to the same conclusion.

"I only stayed with them for a year. They told me I had to go to Israel, to stay with my aunt. My life was upside down and I couldn't do anything to stop their madness. They sent me to Israel to live with an aunt and uncle who had grown children. What did they want a young child for?

"I was not happy when they sent me to live in a Kibbutz. There were so many orphaned children in Israel, at that time. I wanted to live in a home, with a family, not an institution. When my aunt came to visit me, I told her I would not stay! I cried and begged her to take me to her home. She could not refuse me.

"Life with them was not easy; it was a home with two adults who thought they were finished with childrearing. I was not welcomed with open arms. I was taken in." Yael sat motionless now, quietly looking down at the two fragile pieces of paper.

Bobby's mother hadn't kept these two documents; Joseph had them in his possession when he died. Yet like Joseph, Elzbieta never lost her emotional connection to her adopted daughter. Almost eleven years after the kidnapping, when Yael was finally "of age," Elzbieta located her in Israel and, through an intermediary, contacted her daughter. It was during Elzbieta's trip to Israel to visit Yael that she learned what had happened after Yael was taken from the school. In turn, Yael was finally able to hear how friends, family, and networking had helped Elzbieta find Yael's abductors and talk to them. They had been adamant about Elzbieta not seeing Yael again, and Elzbieta finally agreed that she would have no contact with her child. Elzbieta had suffered the loss hoping they were right, that this would be easier for Yael in her new life with blood relatives.

Sitting across a tiny café table in the Jewish Museum, overwhelmed by admiration as well as a growing affection for Bobby's sister, I smiled at Yael and reached for her hands. I realized how much she reminded me of Elzbieta — the part of Elzbieta that Yael still possessed a lifetime later: the life-seeking spirit entreating Yael to make herself strong. Yael emerged intact, a double survivor, most likely with the help of her late husband Oded and the gift of creating her own family — five daughters and the eight grandchildren they have brought into this world.

Several months would pass before my telephone conversation with Yael, focusing again on her separation from Elzbieta. After reading my early draft of her story, Yael needed to set things "right" — to tell another side of the story — and clarify the truth. Her emotional and carefully articulated preface to another perspective of the separation was protective of all parties involved:

"Everyone thought that they were doing things the 'right' and 'good' way," she began. "Now we can say that it was good or not good, but then, then I believe they acted the 'right' way. After all, I was lucky that everyone who took care of me did it with love and good intentions. It is why I think I grew up normal and good and could make a good family."

Yael, speaking from her home in Israel, continued her story. Looking through the precious mementos of her childhood she had found a letter from a relative in France written twelve years or so ago, after Yael had paid what must have been an emotional visit to her family in Paris. Writing in Yiddish, her cousin told the story of how he had found her, as he remembered it — how she came to be separated from Elzbieta. Yael added that she couldn't read the Yiddish, but found someone to translate the letter.

"When Elzbieta and Joseph took me from Warsaw to Paris after the war, it meant going to another country, with another language and customs. It was not easy taking a six-year-old with them," she continued.

Sitting at my dining room table in Long Island, I closed my eyes and tried to imagine Yael sitting across from me, seeking to make things "right."

"They couldn't care for me when we settled in Paris. I did not live with Elzbieta and Joseph in their apartment. They put me in a 'children's home,' a special home for Jewish children near Paris. I was not happy being away from them, but I understood that they could not take care of me.

"In the meantime my uncle — my father's older brother — was living in Israel and found out that I had survived. He managed a newspaper in Israel and had contacts with people who helped him find me. He wrote to Zatrzebie, my last known location, and the people there told him where he could find Elzbieta. Elzbieta had given them her new address. My uncle asked the cousin in Paris to act on his behalf and contact Elzbieta; my cousin did as he asked."

In his letter, Yael's cousin explained that he had contacted Elzbieta and she agreed to let him accompany her during a visit with Yael in the children's home. A short time later, he noted, Elzbieta and Yael visited him and his family in their home. Yael had a hard time remembering the exact sequence of the events that followed. I couldn't tell if it was the challenge of finding English for the concepts she understood in Hebrew, or that she could not make sense of what she had been told.

"Elzbieta took me to their home and left me there to visit with my family. She said she would be back, she would come for me. My cousin said that when Elzbieta came to pick me up I didn't want to go with her. I didn't want to go back to the children's home. I wanted to live with family. My cousin wrote that Elzbieta decided to let me stay with them; Elzbieta left and I did not see her again until I was grown and living in Israel."

Yael finished her new story, and then I mentioned how it differed from the story she had told me months before, as we sat in the café at the Jewish Museum.

"I told you the story as I remembered it," she said with a desperate soft cry choking back her voice. "It was the pain I had felt as a child."

I understood the gratefulness Yael so clearly felt for her family's care through the years, and her deep-felt responsibility for honoring their image — for guiding how others might view their actions. I bowed to Yael's addendum, including both conflicting perspectives of events leading to her separation from Elzbieta. I understood that Yael's family legacy was at stake — that she could not ignore even a possibility that things did not happen just as she and Marian had described them. It was immediately after the war and people did what they thought was "right," she had reminded me, once again.

In pondering the arrangements Elzbieta had made for Marian to stay at Zatrzebie, I realize it makes sense that she would reach out for help providing a safe and healthy environment for Yael — especially if her resources and non-working hours were limited. I knew from Bobby that he had stayed in a residential school as a young child, while Elzbieta was trying to support herself and take care of him as well as her father Israel, who now required nursing care.

The truths of Yael's childhood abduction are embedded within the three narratives — Marian's, Yael's, and the letter written by Yael's cousin. Yet it is Yael who confronted the gut-wrenching truth. The survivors did the best they could to care for each other after the war. Sometimes that meant making choices we can never understand.

Paris, 1950

Elzbieta walked into the beautifully maintained stone schoolhouse, looking forward to yet another joy filled after-noon. She would stop at the market on the way home and

have Yael help her pick out some fresh produce for dinner.
She had no idea how her life was about to change. She had
no idea how her very core, which had survived the war
intact and, perhaps, become even stronger from her war
experiences, would soon be fractured.

Elzbieta didn't see Yael among the children waiting for
their parents. She approached the teacher, who suddenly
looked confused and terribly anxious. The young instructor
tried to explain to Elzbieta that Yael's family had come to
the school and, offering proof of their identity and Yael's,
had removed her from their care. Elzbieta heard the words,
but could not bring herself to acknowledge them. Her natu-
ral contagious smile distorted and the scream that began
deep in her chest ripped through her throat and into the air
between them. "Where is my child?" Elzbieta heard her
own words echo through her brain. These were the same
words she had somehow managed not to hear in the middle
of the night — in her nightmares of the Ghetto and the
sounds of pain and inexplicable loss.

She reached for something to hold on to as she felt her
legs fold beneath her. "Where is my child?" she repeated,
not hearing the responses that administrators tried so hard
to articulate — to explain with an air of certitude, without
revealing their fears of repercussions. "How could you give
my child away?" Elzbieta said, now whispering as she made
an effort to compose herself, to think clearly, so she could
know what to do.

Walking home through the maze of streets that brought
her, somehow, to their apartment, Elzbieta worked hard to
make a plan. She would contact the cousins who took Yael.
She would petition for a hearing and fight for her child —

if not for custody, at least for the right to see her child.

Elzbieta gathered her strength as she entered the apartment. Hands shaking, she wiped her face, trying to restore the composure she needed to bring the news to her father. Much as expected she found Israel quietly working in the apartment, cutting a pair of pants from a pattern he had placed atop fabric draped over the kitchen table. "Papa," she began, trying to slow her speech as her mind raced to some acceptable outcome. "They took Yael. They took my baby."

Elzbieta slumped into a chair as Israel desperately tried to calm Joseph, who, hearing Elzbieta's cries from the bedroom, was now pacing wildly back and forth through the apartment. Elzbieta looked around the apartment, noticed every little toy and article of clothing that lay just as it had when the day had begun, before Yael was taken.

"If the cousins thought they were right," Elzbieta said, repeating these words to herself, as if the logic would help her understand what she should do, "they would not have kidnapped her. They would have met with us and come to some agreement."

"Of course, child," Israel said, caressing his daughter's head. "They knew they were wrong, but that is not the issue now. We must do what is best for the child."

He looked at his beautiful daughter and thought how young she still looked. Her embroidered sweater with the collar of her blouse forming a crisp contour around her face made her look like a student, still making her studies in University. It pained him to see his daughter so tormented by the insensitivity of people who knew what it was to lose loved ones. The Elzbieta who had survived the war with such emotional strength was struggling to control her trembling body. Israel knew that her reactions showed the heart-wrenching complexity of this crisis.

As disgusted as Israel was, he knew there was no right answer, only the best answer for the child's sake. He could not control his thoughts: his compassion for Yael's family; what he would have done to retrieve his sons if they had only been taken away from him and not been killed; and what he would have been capable of doing to simply see Menache's smile one more time. It was no use to plan a counterattack. If only they could arrange to see Yael and say good-bye — let her know that they loved her. Yael needed to know that they had not abandoned or betrayed her. She needed to know that they must let her family raise her and love her too, for the sake of her lost parents.

Elzbieta nodded as Israel revealed his thoughts. She knew deep in her heart that she would have to suffer through this for the sake of her child. They were beyond arguing what was right.

Joseph had a more difficult time coming to terms with Yael's loss. He was suffering, once again, the losses he had suffered through the war. Elzbieta understood this, but it did not make it any easier to help him. Joseph was inconsolable and very, very angry. The war had been a collective injustice, but this was different: this was happening to him. "They came like the Nazis," he said, raising his voice along with his fists. "Like cowards, they came and stole her, like cowards!" Joseph's voice had a strangeness about it that frightened Elzbieta.

"Shah! Shah!" she said, shouting as if she had to wake Joseph up from a nightmare. "It is not the same thing. Yael is alive. She is safe. She will grow to be a woman! It is not the same thing. We have to do what is right for her right now. We cannot pull her away again."

"What's right, what's just, is for me to go steal her back. She is my child!" Joseph sat and cried, cried like a child himself, a lost and enraged child.

Elzbieta knew that Joseph was packing this latest trauma of loss into an emotional space with so much other unspeakable loss — the deaths of his mother, Leon and his family, and the untimely loss of his brother Stanislaw from leukemia, so many years before. His despair was frightening to see, let alone live with. They argued over the decision, day after day, fighting until there was nothing else they could say to one another.

9

Life Anew, 1950-62

"All the art of living lies in a fine mingling of letting go and holding on."

– Henry Ellis

"The world is not comprehensible, but it is embraceable: through the embracing of one of its beings."

– Martin Buber

"They planned on emigrating to Canada," Marian had told me, explaining the sequence of events leading up to his father Israel's death in 1952. "My father had a new business plan: I was in my twenties by now, and he had me look into farmland in Canada — he had read an article about the potential for making a lot of money farming particular crops, 'kay? He had applied for a visa and the physical examination was part of the procedure. That is when they found the cancer."

Elzbieta told Bobby very little about her life in France after the war; she never described her losses or the way she experienced them. I can only imagine what she actually went through — how she reasoned through situations, how she suffered and still managed to look life and death straight in the eye, and go on. As it happened Elzbieta nursed Israel herself, selling her business to stay by his side through the struggle with cancer. With her marriage to Joseph irreparable after Yael's disappearance, and now emotionally and physically drained by her losses and Israel's terminal illness, Elzbieta began the task of supporting her family and rebuilding her life, once again.

After Israel's death Elzbieta considered her options — to stay in France with her brother Adam and their close circle of friends, or succumb to Joseph's persistent requests for her to leave France and emigrate to North America. Joseph urged Elzbieta to come to Canada, where he had settled along with his sister Danka and her family — even promising to grant her the divorce she had requested if she acquiesced. He eventually compromised, agreeing to grant a divorce if she just came to the United States. Elzbieta decided to join Marian in New York.

Bobby remembers precious little of their life in France: of the brief years in the tiny apartment on Rue Breton, and their departure for the United States at age seven. He once told me that he lived in a children's home in Malmaison for a period, but remembered little more than the home's huge, chateau-like appearance, waking up at night in a bunk bed with other children around him, and having the number "72" stitched into all his clothing. It was not an unpleasant memory, the "Chateau" in Malmaison.

Marian had little more detail to offer. "The school was run by a Jewish organization — a Zionist group," he would tell me. "They hoped to prepare the young students for a life in Palestine. I remember visiting Bobby at the school. He was still in a carriage when Elsa first arranged for him to stay there. She had so much to do and take care of; she couldn't give him the attention he needed twenty-four hours a day. She did the best she could," he had added, with noticeable pain in his strained voice. Looking back, Marian could only be defensive of the way they had lived.

Bobby's precious few memories lent additional insight into the life they left behind in Paris. "The apartment was in a very poor part of the city. I recall having to share a communal bathroom. It was very unpleasant walking down the hallway and a flight of steps to the bathroom, which, I can clearly remember, was disgusting. When I returned to France for the first time in the summer of 1966, I found out that our old neighborhood had been quarantined and then leveled.

I was disappointed not to find some remnants of my life there. The fact that the neighborhood had been so badly neglected, so poor and unsuitable for anyone to live in, made it sadder for me," Bobby added.

"Mom hired a tutor for me before we left, so I could learn some English and prepare for our new home. I remember the teacher's perfume, not her face or her name; she must have been one of the teachers at my school. It's amazing how the smell of her perfume stayed with me and, on more than one occasion, has brought her presence to mind. Mom must have studied English as well; I recall her practicing the sound of English words with me.

"I also remember living for a while with a family in Palaiseau, a southern suburb of Paris. Mom arranged for me to stay there to keep me out of the city. I had had a positive reaction to the test for tuberculosis bacterium, which meant that I had been exposed to the disease. Mom wanted me to have a healthy place to play and breathe, so she found a family to take care of me just outside the city. They had a dog named Jimmy. I loved him so much. When I went back to France when I was in high school, the woman — I can't remember her name — met us at the airport. I asked her about Jimmy. She told me he had died a few weeks before we arrived. Isn't that something? I almost saw him again!

"I remember being frightened to leave my life in France. I had few possessions — we must have been so very poor — but I did have to pick some things to take with us. I don't remember what I chose, what was important, but I do remember having to make choices. We sailed on the *Liberté*. She seemed so huge! I also remember being really seasick during the trip.

"I can still recall how the sight of the Statue of Liberty moved Mom. She was visibly awed by the symbol of acceptance in New York's harbor. The tears in her big blue eyes as she held her hands to her chest and sighed frightened me, even as the promise of safety and adventure excited me," Bobby added, wiping an insistent tear from his own face.

Bobby's recollection made me remember the two of us sailing around the Statue of Liberty many years later, when we made our maiden voyage in our current sailboat the *Elize*. We were enthralled by the view of the statue from our little boat. Bobby was drawn back to the first time he had seen the iconic woman.

With seven-year-old Bobby in tow, Elzbieta arrived in New York in April 1956. She had a new "American" moniker, Elizabeth, and hoped to make a new life in the home Marian had prepared for the three of them to share — a one-bedroom apartment on West Seventy-second Street.

"I remember visiting our relatives in Buffalo shortly after our arrival," Bobby says. "It was the first time I met Mom's aunts, Dora and Pearl, and her Uncle Sam. Mom kept in touch with them but we didn't see them too often. Mom worked as a nurse's aide and then in Macy's as a salesperson. I remember her going to classes to learn English. It was difficult for her, but she practiced and practiced, trying to lose her accent." Bobby's remark reminded me of one of his stories of childhood in New York, and how he was embarrassed by his mother's accent.

"Mom had so many friends in New York. Irene and Joseph Griffin, my godparents, were here, and Mom met so many people from Poland, refugees and survivors like herself. Marian told me Mom always had a houseful of friends — a family of friends — around her. She met my stepfather David shortly after we got here and then they married. Marian and Carol must have married around the same time."

Bobby now spent several summers at sleep-away camps in the Laurentian Mountains, just two hours from Joseph's apartment in Montreal. As Bobby approached his teens, summer visits with his father ended and he attended Boy Scout Camps in the States with his friends. He saw Joseph only infrequently, and Joseph seemed content with the arrangements. There was no question he loved his son, Bobby reflected, with sadness in his warm brown eyes, but Joseph's displays of affection were the only memories of their familial tie. Joseph was not the kind of father a young boy could approach baring his soul with his deepest feelings and needs.

"My father's stories about his own life and work always highlighted the amazing, rarely the mundane. He introduced me to business people in Montreal, but rarely to just a good friend. I learned to accept the relationship, limited as it was. Asking for more was pointless, or, on rare occasions, painful," Bobby added. Demonstrative gestures of love were enough for Joseph, so they became enough for Bobby.

I met Bobby's father Joseph only a few times before 1984, the year that he died. He was a bear of a man, who lavished hugs and kisses on our family. I never had a serious conversation with him. He kept his visits to New York light, filled with picture taking, smiles, and gifts for each of his three grandchildren. Just after Joseph's death Bobby flew to his apartment in Montreal and carefully packed up everything that seemed of value — the photographs, documents, and artwork. The scrolled papers so important to Yael were in a cardboard tube covered with brown wrapping paper, nestled in a drawer. Bobby filled Joseph's aging green Oldsmobile with everything he could fit in it and, looking back at the barren apartment that had been Joseph's home, realized how little he had really known about his father — how little Joseph's possessions revealed.

Years later in the summer of 2010, I would with Bobby's blessing open the faded brown files Joseph had kept for decades, to find newspaper clippings and magazine articles, mostly from the early 1960s. The earliest article in Joseph's collection was torn from *Maclean's*, a Canadian magazine, dated March 1, 1954. The article, written by Jack Fishman, was a report on seven Nazi criminals — defendants at the Nuremberg Trials of the International Military Tribunal in 1946. They were all waiting out their sentenced time in Spandau, a prison in Berlin, as the world forgot they existed. Fishman had visited the prison and included recent photographs of each of the seven inmates in his report. The magazine article was published the same year that Elie

Wiesel would begin writing *Night*, describing his experiences in Nazi concentration camps. Wiesel would have a difficult time finding a publisher for his initial manuscript.

Joseph had followed the trial of Nazi war criminal Adolf Eichmann and subsequent articles about Holocaust survivors and the atrocities they endured. He had circled passages with a red pen, adding his reactions to the words describing events and testimonies with exclamation points, the change in the thickness of the red line suggesting the anger he could not and would not abandon.

I myself remember very little about the actual Eichmann trial; I was almost thirteen when it began in 1961, certainly old enough to be aware of world events. I do remember the controversy around Eichmann's abduction in Buenos Aires by the Mossad, Israel's intelligence agency, and his imprisonment in Israel. The trial was my first confrontation with the horrors of the Holocaust; for most of the world, it was delayed acknowledgement of its terrible magnitude.

One of Joseph's numerous faded newspapers following the Eichmann trial was ripped from its binding and stapled along its left edge. A *Bulletin*, published by the Anti-Defamation League of B'Nai Brith in September 1961, answers at least one of the questions forming as I scanned each fragile article on Eichmann's trial: How did the media react to it? The question had been asked in boldface and then answered in the subsequent paragraph: before, and in the week following the start of the trial, American magazines gave substantial space to the subject. Some were editorially opposed to the trial, but *Newsweek*, ostensibly, was more favorably inclined. Once the trial began, the *Bulletin* article suggests, editorial comments became more favorable: yes, the trial was worthy of coverage.

I asked Bobby what he remembered about the trial. "My mother was obsessed with it," he told me, shifting his gaze to a place beyond my left shoulder, as if to find his memories there. "She was glued to the television, pointing at it and voicing her agreement with testimonies. I remember her being so upset, she would sit and cry. It was one of the few times we spoke about the war. She told me that he — Eichmann — and people like him had done terrible things to the Jews. She didn't speak of particulars and I was more upset with her tears than anything. I hated to see her suffer," Bobby said, as I shared the contents of Joseph's precious brown file.

The ADL article also answered another of my questions. How did the general population react to the trial? The most consistent television coverage was a half hour every weeknight on local stations within the New York City radius. The American Broadcasting Company gave the report a prime evening spot and featured tapes of the trial. The ADL said the program attracted a wide audience. In the first days of the trial, ABC offered its New York audience a copy of the full indictment upon request. The station received 10,000 responses the first week, 8,000 the second week, and 6,000 the third. Four weeks after the trial began, NBC covered the trial on Monday evenings from 10 to 11 p.m. and about 180 stations in the country picked up the program. These newscasts devoted spot coverage to the trial, but TV officials apparently felt that "the public was either uninterested or unwilling to watch the resurrected horrors of the Nazi atrocities." No one sponsored a national network show on the trial.

The *Maclean's* article from Joseph's file noted that Israel's newspapers gave a "considerable proportion of their total space to the trial." An ADL survey found that in Israel, sixty percent of the population over age fourteen listened to the radio broadcast of the trial on opening day. The trial had a significant impact on Israel's youth, who for the first time learned what their parents had experienced in Hitler's Europe. In Poland, the press gave the trial extensive documentary reporting and Jewish martyrdom was a dominant theme. These were the words Joseph had needed to save. My heart understood this need.

Also in Joseph's papers, I found an article from the *National Jewish Monthly* dated September 1961. The author, a lawyer and judge in Israel using the pen name E. Davidson, describes how the Eichmann case had the strongest effect on survivors — creating a great catharsis. Memories had been locked up deep inside them for nearly two decades, consciously buried. Israelis who had survived the European hell had started new and productive lives and did not want to see themselves as Eichmann's unresisting victims. When the trial began they began to talk and, most importantly, people listened. Their memories had been released from their buried vaults, bursting forth in the televised tapes of the trial.

In March of 2011, describing the impact of the Eichmann trials on Israelis in *The Eichmann Trial*, Deborah Lipstadt would argue that survivor testimony shattered a distorted image of European Jewry. Israelis had imagined survivors as too meek to defend themselves during the war — an image that contrasted sharply with the self-image of Sabras. During the Eichmann trials Israelis would begin to comprehend the impossibility of resisting the Nazis, thus removing themselves from a position of moral superiority over their Diaspora cousins; Sabras were simply "generationally and geographically lucky," Lipstadt would write.

Joseph's yellowed reports of the trial describe people screaming and crying that they wanted to kill Eichmann, who remained protected in his bulletproof glass box during the trial. The story of how he directed the "final solution" came out into the open for Jews and non-Jews alike to consider and judge. Sitting in my sunny kitchen in 2010, I remembered how Eichmann had asked for understanding and mercy from the Jewish people — claiming that he had acted "under orders," that he had only done as he had been told. The moral and legal responsibility we have for our own actions was what I, as a child, had taken away from the trial.

Stacks of neatly folded newspaper articles, placed in a safe storage place, kept Joseph connected to his own pain. The expressive red markings and underlining appear repeatedly in the newspaper articles Joseph saved from 1964 — articles commemorating the nineteenth anniversary of the liberation of concentration camps by the Canadian Armed Forces.

Elzbieta's suffering did not need to be made real by faded newspaper clippings hidden in a closet. She suffered the memories with each article she read and television broadcast she needed to see. As the media covered the graphic details revealed during the Eichmann trial, Elzbieta endured the testimonies and recollections. She had been satisfied when she watched the news one evening in May 1962 and knew that the State of Israel had put Adolf Eichmann to death by hanging.

Bobby did not question his mother about her own experiences. At age thirteen he could see how the testimony of others had already so deeply affected her. For her own part, Elzbieta did not want her only child to hear the stories she had buried so deep inside. It was enough that she and Marian would have the burden of unforgettable images. She let go of her resurrected anger, moved on with her life, and, whenever possible, she released her huge smile and laughed.

The *Liberté*, April 1956

Elzbieta held Robert's hand a little tighter as she stepped onto the gangway and gazed up at the huge ship. "Regardez, Robert! Regardez la taille de la Liberté. *C'est le plus grand navire que j'ai jamais vu !" Elzbieta hesitated for a moment and continued in English. She needed to practice the new language and Robert needed to hear the English words he had studied. "Look at the size of the ship!*

It is the biggest ship I have ever seen. The Liberté will take us across the sea to America, our new home," she said, trying to lift her voice above the sorrow she felt tightening her throat.

Elzbieta looked into her son's eyes and saw her own mixed emotions shared in his big brown eyes. "It will be good, Robert," she whispered as she pulled a wide grin across her face. "Marian waits for us. We will see him when we get to New York." The mention of Marian brought a smile to Robert's trembling lips. "Tak," Elzbieta sighed to herself, reverting to her native tongue, the language of her deepest emotions. She needed to be so careful with him, she thought. He can sense when I am not being honest. I can see it in his brow, as it begins to crease when he catches me in a moment of despair and I tell him I am all right.

The trip was more difficult than she thought it would be. The sea was turbulent, the waves riding high and crashing against the bow of the ship. She looked to her right, to the row of people lined up against the railing trying to gain composure as the rolling ship played havoc on their stomachs. There were so many people sharing their own stories of pain, disappointment, and the hopes that America would bring a new start. She feared that she was participating in a mass fantasy.

Elzbieta stood on deck looking out at the stretch of blue water, separating her from all she had known in her lifetime. She felt a tightening in her stomach, an all too familiar feeling of stress. "Why am I so anxious?" she asked herself. "I leave nothing behind. My father is gone, my brother Adam is safe in Paris with his wife Krysia and

daughter Louisette — he has a new surname, Rodier, to
mask his Jewish heritage."

She wouldn't miss the fear she had experienced even in
France — the fear of being looked down upon, criticized,
even harmed, because she was a Jew. Much like the other
members of the Jewish community in Paris, she had been
anxious about circumcising Robert. She didn't want him to
be identifiable if it started all over again. Israel hadn't
believed they should hide their heritage. Elzbieta acquiesced.

Marian assured her it was different in America, in
New York. The anti-Semitism may be there, but it is not so
blatant, not so widespread. Why do I feel as though I am
leaving a part of myself behind? she asked herself, and
closed her eyes, allowing her mind to wander. It was the
ribbons — the pink ribbons she kept in her drawer —
that she envisioned. Ahh, she sighed. It is Jadzia, my
precious little girl.

Elzbieta reasoned through her pain, the constant tor-
ment she had to fight when her guard was down, when she
encountered times of uncertainty. Jadzia was no longer in
France. She knew this. Her contacts had informed her that
the child was sent to Israel, to live with an uncle. Elzbieta
could do nothing until Jadzia reached eighteen, then she
would be able to contact her. She had to wait three more
years. She could do that in New York too. Adam had her
contact information in New York if anyone needed to reach
her before then.

"You must trust your instincts," her father said. He had
wanted to go to North America to start a new life. She had
decided to go when he died; she had no choice. Joseph would
grant a divorce if she emigrated to America. It was close

enough to Canada, she had convinced him; he could spend
time with Robert. Elzbieta knew she only needed to stay in
New York a short time. She would return to France once
she had secured the papers. If only she could feel confident
in her plan.

Below in their cabin, Robert stayed in his bed, trying to
reach the bucket in time as nausea overtook him. Elzbieta
held his head as the seasickness rid the child's body of every
morsel of food she managed to encourage him to eat. The
medicine would help, that she knew. She tucked him under
the blanket and watched him gradually fall back to sleep.
America will welcome him, she thought to herself. The chil-
dren will welcome him into their lives and he will have a
normal life, even as a Jew. Marian had told her that
America was . . . What was it?. . . a pot that mixes?. . .
that melts? Robert will be in a pot that mixes all people.
He will be a little boy, just like other little boys.

Elzbieta closed her eyes and envisioned the streets and
avenues of New York, the way Marian had described them.
"There are no scars of the war here," he assured her.
"People will welcome you, even with your accent. They will
let you live and be well," he had written. Elzbieta took a
deep breath and put her head down next to her sleeping
child. "We will live and be well together," she said, ever so
quietly, and, as the ship gently rocked, she fell asleep.

10

Over His Shoulder, 2010

"One of my friends, in the prime of life, spent a night studying
accounts of the holocaust, especially the Warsaw Ghetto. In the morning he
looked at himself in the mirror and saw a stranger:
his hair had turned white. Another lost not his youth but his reason.
He plunged back into the past and remains there still.
From time to time I visit him in his hospital room: we look at one another
and we are silent. One day, he shook himself and said to me:
'Perhaps one should learn to cry.' "

– Elie Wiesel, Holocaust survivor

Sue, you may want to see the article in the *New York Times*. Hope all is well, Marian." Marian's e-mail had surprised me, because I hadn't heard from him for months and hadn't expected him to want to discuss the *Times* article. I knew exactly what Marian wanted me to read — Jeannette Catsoulis's review of Yael Hersonski's new production *A Film Unfinished*. I had seen the article the day before, on August 17, and had planned to travel into Manhattan to see the film. My e-mailed response had been immediate: "I saw the article and want to see the movie. Let me know if you want to come into the city. Love, Susan." Marian didn't respond.

Jeannette Catsoulis had described *A Film Unfinished* as the story of the unmasking of Nazi propaganda: "For almost half a century, an unfinished Nazi propaganda film of the Warsaw Ghetto, simply titled *Das Ghetto* and discovered by East German archivists after the war, was used by scholars and historians as a flawed but authentic record of Ghetto life.

Shot over 30 days in May 1942 — just two months before deportations to the Treblinka extermination camp would begin — the original hour-long silent film juxtaposed random scenes of Jews enjoying various luxuries with images of profound suffering." When another reel was unearthed in 1998 — thirty minutes of outtakes showing the extent to which scenes had been deliberately staged, Catsoulis stated — *Das Ghetto* was subjected to scholars' critical reappraisal.

In the revealing outtakes, well-dressed Jews enter a butcher's shop over and over, ignoring the ragged, starving children begging outside. In another repeated scenario, filmmakers direct prosperous-looking passersby to disregard the corpses abandoned on the sidewalk. With evidence of orchestrated scenes showing extreme heartlessness on the part of wealthy Jews toward their less fortunate neighbors, the propaganda intended for the earlier version became clear. Beyond propaganda, however, the impetus for creating the Nazi film remains as obscure as ever.

Excerpts from a recently a taped interview with Willy Wist, one of the cameramen who worked on *Das Ghetto* and agreed to share his memories for the new film, are as evasive as one might expect. Readings from personal diaries such as those of Adam Cherniakov, the head of the Jewish Council (whose apartment was used by the Nazis to stage several scenes), and from the minutely detailed reports of the Ghetto commissioner Heinz Auerswald, are paired with actual scenes in the Ghetto. The pairings provide vivid insight into the restrictions of daily life and the perverse methods of the Nazi filmmakers.

Other witnesses did not withhold information or commentary. Yael Hersonski's decision to invite five survivors of the Warsaw Ghetto to view the original footage, and to film their reactions for *A Film Unfinished*, underscores what Catsoulis refers to as the "difference between watching and seeing." It provides another layer of understanding, a layer only a subjective witness can expose.

Bobby and I didn't see the film until the end of September, when it arrived at our local Art Cinema. Marian had communicated through his sons that he wanted to see the film with us, but he did not make any plans. Hoping to catch a showing during the only weekend of the film's short stay in our local theater, Bobby called Marian and said he was welcome to join us. Marian was evasive; he would let us know the following week. When he didn't call, Bobby and I saw the film on our own. Both Bobby and I were distressed by the images we saw. The clips of starving and dying children and life going on, alongside omnipresent death, haunted us. How did Elzbieta and Marian manage to keep their eyes on life when death greeted them each morning — its smell and vacant eyes, literally waiting at their doorstep?

I was relieved that Marian was not sitting next to me as I shuddered and cried. Distorted faces of emaciated women and children filled the screen, followed by images of the inevitable consequences: discarded corpses distorted in ways I could not allow myself to see. My instincts took over: I covered my eyes.

Marian called the following Monday to say he would be visiting us the next day. I thought I knew what he would want to do, so I prepared myself to "revisit" the Ghetto.

Marian and his son Ira arrived in mid-afternoon, just in time to spend a few hours with Ella and our daughter-in-law Lisa, who were visiting for the afternoon. Ella was thrilled to see her familiar "friends" and sought out their participation in a game of hide and seek. I had no idea how prescient Ella was in her choice of games.

Bobby spent a quiet evening talking to Marian and Ira while I taught a painting class in my studio. After my class, I was eager to spend a few hours calming my thoughts before going to sleep. I made Marian and Bobby a cup of tea and we sat together engaged in casual conversation. I had not mentioned the film and did not want to initiate conversation about it, but Marian was obviously interested otherwise.

"Sue, is the movie still playing locally?" he asked, as I sat back into the soothing lushness of my living room sofa, warm tea in hand, about to watch one of my favorite television programs.

"Yes," I replied. "As a matter of fact, we can see a show tomorrow afternoon, around 1 p.m., if you'd like, and I'll still have enough time to prepare for my afternoon class."

"Good. I'd like that," he stated without hesitation.

I had a difficult time sleeping that night. Concerned about Marian's response to the movie and how little time I'd have to talk to him afterwards, I couldn't imagine teaching a class immediately after what I anticipated being a disturbing experience for both of us. As I tossed and kicked off my blankets, I made a plan: I would also show Marian a travelogue of Warsaw filmed in 1939, which I had recently purchased from a Jewish film site on the Internet. I had been looking for images of Warsaw before the war when I found it. Studying pictures of Marian's environment before and during the war informed my own re-creations of Marian's stories. I also felt the 1939 film would please Marian, who didn't seem to remember too much about the city. I fell asleep after exhausting myself playing out the numerous ways the events of the following day could unfold.

When I returned home from my early morning activity — babysitting for Ella and then taking her to her pre-school program — I found Marian and Ira awake and ready to begin their day. As I prepared LJ for his morning walk, Marian asked if he could join me: an opportunity to spend some time together, just the "three" of us. This simple act, taking a walk together, was unusual if not absent from the years before "our project" began. I dismissed thoughts of how sad it had been not to have this closeness with Marian all those years, and focused on our precious new relationship.

LJ was eager to take the lead as Marian and I negotiated the mile-and-a-half route through the neighborhood. We talked about how much the enclave, nestled on the North Shore of Long Island, had changed in the thirty-some years Bobby and I had lived here. New construction replaced the understated homes of the professionals who had settled here in the 1950s. Now it was two- and three-story variations of contemporary colonials — their vaulted entrances and multiple, overlapping roofs emphasizing a need for expansive space. I wondered how Marian might remember his Warsaw neighborhood — the streets and buildings of the two films we would see in a matter of hours.

Marian kept pace with LJ and me as we rounded the corner into the last stretch of our route. "I read about the film, 'kay? The original was a propaganda film," he told me, forgetting that I had told him I had seen it already. "They were trying to show the contrast between the wealthy Jews in the Ghetto and the very poor, 'kay?, staging scenes of Jews enjoying their privileged life, ha!, and scenes of the very poor." Marian was referring to the suffocating decrepitude of the poor — their progressing demise from starvation and untreated disease. I didn't want to mention the things that upset me — the starving faces and corpses abandoned by families too poor to pay burial fees that would take food from the living. I decided to wait and let Marian observe what I had "witnessed."

As we approached my street I mentioned the travelogue *A Day in Warsaw*, the one I wanted to share with Marian. I told him how it had given me a better idea of what Warsaw had looked like: the old neighborhoods and the old Synagogue — the one that I knew had managed to survive the war. Marian looked at me with a huge smile on his face.

"I think that's the synagogue where Elzbieta got married! Can we see the film before we go to the theater? I'd love to see it this morning."

I had hoped to give Marian this more positive experience, with joyfully familiar images to ponder, before we visited the Ghetto. So far, so good.

The travelogue had been an unexpected find. In 1938 and 1939,

Shaul and Yitzhak Goskind, of the Warsaw-based production company Sektor Films, produced six travelogues depicting urban Jewish communities in Poland. *A Day in Warsaw*, along with the extant films about Bialystok, Cracow, Lwow, and Vilna (no copy of the Lodz film has been found), retains its original Yiddish narration, supplemented by new English subtitles.

The Jewish neighborhoods in Warsaw, including Zamenhof Street and the commercial area on Nalewki Street, show the multistoried buildings, broad streets, the old market square and Jewish quarter, home to a Hasidic community. Trucks, trolleys, autos, and buses move around and alongside horse-drawn carriages, pushcarts, and porters, moving people and merchandise through the busy streets. Images of the Yiddish Theater, Gensza Cemetery, and the various Jewish institutions — the community council, hospitals, schools and synagogues — flash across the screen. The ten-minute film, which begs the viewer to "push pause" and hold the memory or first encounter just a little bit longer, presents a portrait of a vibrant city and its inhabitants, communities, and institutions. It would be all but obliterated in the handful of years to come.

Marian and I sat on my living room couch as I arranged the television control, digital recorder, and paper and pencil before me on the glass cocktail table. It was the same glass table and mahogany cube base that once sat in Joseph's apartment, along with the marble sculpture of an abstracted lobster that sat in the middle of the table, stabilizing the glass tabletop. We could both see the textured wool of the brightly patterned red and orange kilim beneath the table — the kilim Elzbieta helped me pick out decades ago at Cepelia, the Polish arts and crafts store in Manhattan where she worked when I first met her.

The introduction to the worn and static-laced travelogue appeared on the flat-panel screen on the wall. I adjusted the sound for Marian and both of us sat straight up at the edge of the sofa, as images of old Warsaw appeared no more than ten feet in front of us, across my living room wall. Marian's initial reaction to the film was that the city it captured was unfamiliar terrain.

"I don't remember this, 'kay?" he told me, almost asking if I had something more familiar to show him. I realized, once again, that I was testing the memory of an eighty-year-old man who was only age eight or nine when he might have encountered these parts of the city. It also occurred to me that he might never have visited the city's travelogue sites.

When the camera panned Nalewki Street, Marian grabbed my hand. "I remember that!" he exclaimed. "Pause the film!" he begged of me. "My uncle had a wholesale business there, on Nalewki. He made uppers for shoes." Marian could not remember his uncle's name. "It was in the better part of Warsaw," Marian said, anxious to continue his sightseeing tour.

"Your uncle?" I asked. "How was he related to you?"

"My father had two married sisters who remained in Warsaw when the rest of the family emigrated to the United States."

"Do you remember their names?" I asked, surprised to discover two new family members.

"No, I wish I could."

As the travelogue continued to identify key institutions and commercial establishments, Marian's excitement rose. "Look at that building! Hold it! My father had three stores in that building, *Wielo Pole*! One for himself that my mother worked in, one for Adam, and one for his cousin, 'kay?" I paused the film and studied the curve of the cylindrical building's corner and the wooden columns with diagonal supports lining the building's sides.

"It doesn't look as polished as I remember it." Marian's appraisal of the building's architectural qualities and maintenance infused his voice with a soft sadness. "It was the location of the store for Jews and peasants. He had another store in a very exclusive neighborhood, 'kay?, a wealthy Polish neighborhood. He hired a manager for that store.

We didn't go there. As a matter of fact, he was told not to go there," Marian said, looking at me and nodding to emphasize the stigma attached to stores owned by Jews.

"And that! The indoor market!" he exclaimed. "My father and his brother-in-law had a space there where they stored preserved pears. They kept them until Christmas time, 'kay?, and then they sold them wholesale. They made a lot of money!

"I lived a few blocks away — at 4 Ptasia Street," he said, smiling. Earlier, Marian had not remembered the address of his childhood home. After the war he had filled out a form requiring his address in 1939 and he listed it as Ptasia Street, No.4. I had found a copy of the form in the archives of the Jewish Historical Institute and included it in the draft of his story — the one he had recently read. Marian's smile had been a nod of thanks.

As the gray-toned images of Warsaw appeared on my television screen, Marian tried to recognize something else, anything else. "Look! Pause the film! That statue of the Polish King, Zygmundt. I remember when it lay in the streets, after the Germans bombed Warsaw in 1939. The monument toppled from its base, 'kay?, but wasn't destroyed. They wanted to save it. I remember riding my bicycle around it!

"And there, the Savings and Loan, my father used to go every week. I remember that building. Wait, look at that — the synagogue! Elzbieta was married in that synagogue! I remember it being very fancy," Marian said as he studied the entrance to the Nozhik Synagogue — the one we both knew had survived the war.

"We didn't go there for services. They had a cantor and assigned seats there. The Nozhik Synagogue was a place to have a beautiful wedding. Our shul, which was more modest, had been destroyed."

As the narrator noted bustling Jerusalem Avenue, with its buses and horse and buggies, Marian told me he had lived there for six months. "When was that?" I asked, not knowing where to place this residence on our timeline. "Was it before Stasio was taken?"

"No," Marian replied. "Stasio was long gone. It was during the autumn of 1943." It was at this moment that Marian told me how he and Elzbieta had escaped from the Gestapo through the back stairs of the apartment they had shared with the kind Polish woman.

Marian and I had seen the travelogue twice and it was getting late. Ira returned from his dental appointment with Bobby, the other reason they had come downstate for the visit, and I prepared a quick lunch before we left to see *A Film Unfinished*. I was happy we had a chance to view the film about Warsaw first — that Marian had enjoyed seeing that which no longer remains.

I tried to make casual conversation as I served the eggplant parmigiana I had prepared in advance, anticipating a quick lunch. Marian and Ira questioned me about the recipe for a dish they were clearly savoring; Ira, who had been preparing some simple meals at home, seemed eager to learn how to cook the tasty entree. Marian confided that with arthritis his wife Carol was finding it difficult to stand at the stove cooking, so he and his two sons had been taking over the kitchen. I penned the recipe before we left the house.

We arrived at the local cinema just as the feature started. It was 1:10 in the afternoon and there were only three other people in the theater. I found myself more conscious of Marian, sitting beside me, than of the now familiar distressing images flashing across the screen. I didn't know how Marian would react to the stories of the survivors interviewed in the film — survivors who were viewing the original film as we watched them in *A Film Unfinished*.

I watched Marian's reaction out of the corner of my eye. He held his hands up to his face, as if holding his cheeks in place. I heard no sounds besides the sound track's pronounced clicking as the original Nazi film was depicted moving through the projector. I couldn't wait for the film to end; two times was one more than I could bear.

Exiting the theater, I let Marian take the lead. He was quiet as we walked to the car. I waited for him to speak, but he did not.

"I know the Nazis manipulated the scenes to show the contrast between the Ghetto's inhabitants, the rich and the poor, but I'm not sure how much was staged," I said, softly engaging Marian.

"It was a propaganda film and the cameraman knew what was going on. How could he not!" Marian replied. He was referring to the reenactment of cameraman Willy Wist's testimony before the West German government, which had prosecuted war criminals in the 1960s. In the film Wist could not convince his interrogators, years later, that he did not know that the suffering human beings he was filming were starving to death at the hands of his own people.

"He was as guilty as the people who sent him there. He knew what was going on," Marian repeated. After seeing the film I couldn't help but agree.

"We saw them filming. Elzbieta and I saw them filming, but from a distance," he said then. "She told me not to go near them. They were grabbing anyone who was well-dressed to participate in the film and she was afraid I'd go too close!"

I mentioned a scene in *A Film Unfinished* that had been especially upsetting to see:

"One of the survivors shown viewing the original film described a time she had tripped over a body in the street and, for the first time, felt the terror she had been able to side-step and ignore." The woman had hidden her face as the images flashed on her viewing screen: corpses lying on the streets and men attending to the dead by putting them in wooden boxes or simply piling them onto carts and carrying them away to the cemetery to be added to the piles in mass graves. "I cannot look at it," she had cried, trying to hide her eyes and yet view the horror, as if for the first time. "I cannot look, now that I have my humanity," she sobbed, acknowledging that her experiences in the

Ghetto had forced her to turn away from the sight of death, from the daily assault on her sense of human decency.

"Was it true that people just walked around corpses left on the street — left outside in the open because their families couldn't afford funerals?" I asked Marian, thinking that this too may have been staged.

"Yes, I walked past the bodies, 'kay? I could not look. If I did, I saw my own face. I saw what could happen to me. We had to survive. To look at the bodies was to see yourself, what could happen to you. I couldn't look. I had to survive."

I was suddenly pulled from the moment to the written words of Primo Levi, the chemist-turned-writer Auschwitz survivor. Levi, in *The Drowned and the Saved*, writes about the experience of shame that coincided with the end of the war and regained freedom:

> *"Coming out of the darkness, one suffered because of the reacquired consciousness of having been diminished. Not by our will, cowardice, or fault, yet nevertheless we had lived for months and years at an animal level: our days had been encumbered from dawn to dusk by hunger, fatigue, cold, and fear, and any space for reflection, reasoning, experiencing emotions were wiped out. We endured filth, promiscuity, and destitution, suffering much less than we would have suffered from such things in normal life, because our moral yardstick had changed."*

The ethical compass of the Jews, carrying its strong, irresistible pull to the "right behavior" and "the good" for generations upon generations, had lost its absolute direction, wavering with each decision needed for one's own survival. Marian had held back so much of the story of his life during and after the war — he had to. So much was inconceivable to us today.

"Did you listen to what her mother did when she ran home crying?" Marian cried out, as we walked across the theater's parking lot, bringing me back to the moment. "Her mother gave her bread and jam and told her to shush, 'kay? They had bread and jam! That's not how it was! We were hungry all the time. No one had enough food. I'm not talking about just being hungry. I felt the constant pain that starvation brings. The butchers and their meat — the ones they showed in the movie. I never saw that in the Ghetto!"

Marian was referring to the film's scenes depicting butcher shops with their delicacies hanging in their windows and restaurants with ample amounts of food piled high on the dishes of their festive, well-heeled customers.

"It was a propaganda film," I reminded him as we belted ourselves into the seats of my car. Marian was caught up in his anger, his unthinking response to the movie, and the surge of emotions he was now able to feel. Reasoning with him became difficult and we drove home in silence, unhurriedly.

Once we returned to my home Marian and Ira found comfortable seats on the patio and thumbed through the newspaper, as they enjoyed the warm fall air. Marian was calmer now. I sat with them for a few minutes, attempting to compose myself, before I went to work.

"Sue," Marian began, "I enjoyed the film of Warsaw — the one we saw this morning. It was amazing how I remembered the building where my father had his stores. That was good."

I looked at his smiling face and saw his delight in memories of the long-forgotten familiar sights. I was so happy we had watched *A Day in Warsaw*. Marian had a pleasant experience to reflect upon, to hold onto when he and Ira made their way home that evening — even as he buried the images of the Ghetto, once again.

I had Marian's smile to dwell on that day and much more in the months to come. Seven months later, in the early spring of 2011 when Bobby sat at our kitchen table showing Marian his new iPad, Marian was eager to use the new technology to navigate his way through virtual streets of contemporary Warsaw. We shared his excitement.

"This is the building, 4 Ptasia Street — I see the courtyard and the adjacent corner of the street!" Marian spoke with delight as he brushed his fingers along the surface of the screen, moving the image to the right and then to the left, and then multiplying in magnification with each outward flick of his fingers.

"Here is the park I used to play at! Can you imagine! I used to go there with Menache."

Some of the technology that let Marian "walk" down the streets of Warsaw had been available for years, but Marian's desire — and ability — to do so had just recently emerged, after two years of painful digging.

Apparently spurred by his newly freed memories, Marian now found the strength to search his cache of mementos for an image of his brother Leon. On one visit Marian tenderly handed me a small photograph of Rivka, Israel, and Leon. It was the first image of Leon I had seen, and it was comforting to see, at last, the face of Marian's brother.

"I think it may have been taken at my brother Adam's wedding," Marian explained.

In the photograph Rivka appears caught in a moment of clowning, making faces, even as Leon and Israel dutifully look toward the photographer. It was not a flattering picture of Rivka. I thought about Elzbieta's reluctance before the camera in the years that I knew her and how we always seemed to catch her talking to us and not smiling. "Smile for the camera," Bobby would coax her, only to have her make a funny face and send the children into fits of laughter. Elzbieta disliked being the object of a photographic lens. Was it a woman's vanity? I thought about all those unflattering pictures taken of me through the years, and how I could possibly protect my image for posterity, choosing which ones to keep and which to destroy — as if I could do such a thing. How would Rivka feel about this picture surviving and being one of the two unflattering pictures of her as an adult to survive through the ages? She didn't expect it would be. It occurred to me that if Rivka had smiled, even in one of the pictures, Elzbieta wouldn't have needed the Styka painting.

I added a copy of the newly unearthed portrait of Rivka, Leon, and Israel to my digital collection of family pictures. Cropping the image, I created an enlarged version of Leon's face for Marian to keep. Holding the surprisingly unfamiliar image in his hands, Marian quietly studied Leon's features.

"I always thought that Leon had resembled my father," he whispered, with some difficulty. Clearing his throat, Marian looked up at me and smiled.

"I can see now that Leon looked like Elsa." What a fond discovery, I felt. What a fine outcome of our "project."

Later that spring I would also send Marian several chapters of this book and ask him to check the accuracy of the stories. His phone conversation was energized, enthusiastic. New memories would also surface from the written words.

"Sue, I finished checking the manuscript last night and wanted to tell you some things I jotted down," he began.

"You must have been up all night reading," I teased, knowing he had received the envelope Monday afternoon and it was now Wednesday morning.

"Yes I was," he laughed. "You know, it bothered me that I couldn't remember the German Jewess's name. I should have remembered her. She was so beautiful and so good to me, 'kay? Yes, she saved my life when I was selected for deportation, but she always treated me well — like a kid brother. I was reading the story and her name came to me: Paula! Paula Warszawska! We were very close; I don't know how I ever forgot her name. She even invited me to her wedding!" Marian said, with clear delight in recalling her precious name and associated events.

"When did she get married?" I asked, assuming it was after 1943 and on the Aryan side. Marian's story would prove me wrong.

"In December, December of 1942," he replied.

"In the Ghetto?"

"Yes, in the Ghetto. Can you imagine? She married Benjamin Rutman's relative! They met in the Ghetto. He worked in the factory where she worked, in Toebbens, at 12 Prosta Street. Paula worked directly for Herr Bauch, the German director of the factory. She was such a beautiful woman that Bauch had her sit in the front office. The German officers would come in and ask her if she was a Jew. She never denied being Jewish. 'Then why aren't you wearing your badge?' the Germans would ask, teasing as much as taunting. 'Herr Bauch does not permit it,' she would tell them, asserting that she knew it would otherwise be a punishable offense not to wear her badge.

"The Germans in the office were good to me, personally, 'kay? I was not mistreated. They had me collect information from sites all over the Ghetto, from places where they did not have phones. They needed to understand what the workshops had produced and what they had shipped. When I think of the fortunes they made using slave labor!" he exclaimed.

"I even spoke to Paula on the phone, after I left. She eventually told me it was not safe for us to speak. That was the last I heard of her," he added, wistfully.

"Did she survive?"

"I don't believe so," Marian responded. He also revealed that his recent sleepless night had been mixed with the joys of his recollections as well as their pain.

"How old was she?" I asked, realizing I had thought of Paula as middle-aged when Marian had first described her as a German Jewess. Now, knowing she had married in the Ghetto, it occurred to me she was probably younger, much younger.

"I believe she was in her mid to late twenties. I don't know exactly how old she was," Marian responded, with apology for not having more to offer.

"Did Elsa have a close relationship with Paula too?" I asked, expecting a sense of family engendered by friendship with a woman the same age, and Paula's marriage to Benjamin's relative.

"I have no recollection of Elsa having a close relationship with Paula. I would see them occasionally talking to each other during working hours, 'kay? I assumed it was work related, not personal. Elsa did not attend — was not invited to — Paula's wedding. But she always spoke of Paula with affection."

Marian surprised me with his recollections of Paula. In my mind she was an older woman in the office where he worked. Surprisingly, she had been willing to risk her own safety by naming Marian as "valuable," and challenging the Germans selecting him for deportation. In fact, she had been a close friend. That their bond did not include Elzbieta was also a surprise. Marian was twelve at the time and would naturally be enthralled by a beautiful woman who obviously cared for him — especially one coveted by grown men and even Jew-hating German soldiers. I can imagine that Marian's feelings for Paula, whether or not becoming a teen "crush," could have been powerful. Perhaps they even fueled his seemingly emboldened trek out of the Ghetto.

Marian had been able to sift through the horrific and the unspeakable: to find, at last, the feelings of loving and being loved and cared for, even as he had felt the hatred and disgust of those powerful German soldiers, the men who deemed him worthless, deserving only death.

Elzbieta may have witnessed Marian's renewed energy pulling him out of the grieving for his mother and brother. Perhaps she would not have discouraged any relationship that gave him strength, infused him with passion and the will to stay alive. Elzbieta needed Marian to work hard at living through the oppressive last months in the Ghetto, and the challenging days to come. She needed him to survive, to be ready, when the time came, to make his way from Ghetto life and beyond to the uncertainty of existence on the Aryan side. Marian's survival must have strengthened Elzbieta in her own struggle to live through these days.

Several months before Marian had remembered Paula, I was in my studio one day, in the winter of 2011. I wasn't teaching a class — I was painting. I was working on a portrait of Elzbieta, loosely based on an old sepia photograph taken in her late twenties, juxtaposed with a mind's eye image of her walking down a street. I wasn't sure whether the surrounding buildings were in Poland, Paris, or New York. Actually it didn't matter where they were; Elzbieta had always had a wonderful stride — evident in the early photograph of her walking down a street in Warsaw before the war. I needed to capture this recurring imagery. It was how I wanted to remember her, to depict her for people who didn't know her, as well as those who did. I must have been successful. . . .

Ella and her mother Lisa joined me in the studio as Lisa prepared for her afternoon class. She had been teaching in my pre-school art program and Ella, nearly four, fashioned herself Lisa's assistant, helping set up the easels. Ella sat herself at one of the easels, having a snack before she began her work — placing six tubes of paint at each easel. She hesitated for a moment as she looked up at me working on the canvas, which was hanging on my work wall in the back of the studio.

"Nana?" she called, pulling my attention to her and away from the canvas. "Nana, who is the lady — the lady with my daddy's eyes?"

Ella had noticed the resemblance between her father Adam and his grandmother Elzbieta. This legacy of Elzbieta's genes had startled all of the family as I first began to sketch in the features from the sepia photograph. Now tiny Ella had seen it too.

None of us had seen Elzbieta's youthful face mirrored in Adam's when we found the photograph, shortly after Elzbieta passed away over ten years before. We didn't realize that Adam would mature — now at thirty-two — to look so much like her. Ella saw the eyes and recognized their shape and color: they belonged to her daddy. Frankly, with Elzbieta's hair piled on top of her face, and with her strong cheekbones and broad forehead, everyone thought the portrait was of Adam.

"That is Elzbieta, your daddy's grandma," I said to my little granddaughter. "That is who you are named for, where your name came from: Ella Jane came from your daddy's grandma Elzbieta, and your mommy's grandma Betty Jane."

Ella sat very still, the gaze of her own version of Elzbieta's eyes moving between me and the painting. Lisa turned aside for a moment, hiding her tears, and listened to the beginning of a story. . . .

Epilogue: Stasio

In mid-spring of 2011, I had called Uncle Marian to discuss a delicate situation. We were well along in our updating — sharing recent family activities — when Marian began a story about his arrival in the United States, at age twenty. It was not a new story, or new in information for our project, but we had found a ripe moment within our banter — suddenly, my gift of the chance to ask a question long needing an answer:

"Marian, when you came to America to live with your aunts and uncles in Rochester, did they know what you had been through? What had happened to the family?"

"They knew as much as they had been told and had read in the papers," he replied, "but no, they had no idea what had actually happened. And, I did not speak of it." Thus was acknowledged his history of silence, and his lack of emotional support as he settled into life in America.

"My dad died shortly after I was recruited into the army, in 1952. I had just left Rochester for training when I learned that Israel had died in Paris. He didn't last very long once lung cancer was diagnosed. He went quickly. I couldn't leave or do anything. The rabbi at the army base spent some time with me and they gave me a few days off, but I was by myself," Marian added, reflectively.

Today's world — a world sensitive to the effects of traumatic stress — knows that Marian's lack of support, the absence of interactive soothing, hurt him deeply. Yet after World War II, I would learn, social workers typically urged Holocaust survivors to forget their horrific experiences and get on with their lives. Thus Marian's silence until the first of our conversations, seeking to remember, wanting to forget.

I turned the conversation gently in a new direction. Marian had given me a white cardboard box containing Elzbieta's extraordinary book the *Album of Pictures*, and I had only recently opened it up to look more carefully at the images as well as the text. As I lifted the album out of its plain cardboard casket, I noticed a piece of white paper on the bottom of the box. I retrieved the lonely paper and turned it over only to find the words Yad Vashem, in bold capital letters, printed across the top left corner. It was the application form for the Holocaust Martyrs' and Heroes' Remembrance Authority — the Testimony Guide Sheet I had given to Uncle Marian some months before. I didn't know what to make of Marian placing the Testimony Sheet in with the *Album of Pictures*. If he had done it unintentionally, he would have asked me for it again — to replace the mislaid copy. If he had forgotten about it, perhaps I hadn't made a strong enough case for Stanislaw Drabik's status as one of the Righteous Among the Nations. On the other hand, Marian could have left it in the box for me to fill out for him. Bobby wasn't so sure the form's placement was an oversight.

"I don't think he wants to pursue the nomination," Bobby said as he handled the guide sheet. Looking up into my eyes, his own brown eyes held a sadness born years before I ever met him. "It's enough that he has given us his story, a story I never would have had if it hadn't been for our Ella, for our family. Marian doesn't need to relive this for strangers in Jerusalem. Let's be happy with what we have. It has not been without negative consequences; Marc told me Marian has been having nightmares. Let's let it be."

I thought about Bobby's reaction and hesitated to begin this conversation with Marian. When he mentioned dealing with his father's death without comfort from a family member, I wanted to remind him that he was no longer alone in his re-creations: we were there for him now. I needed to ask if he wanted me to help him.

"Marian, I found the application form for Yad Vashem in the box you left with me. Did you want some help filling it out?"

"Please, if you would. I can give them the personal information they request, but I have to write down the story of what actually happened with Stasio. They need facts about his family, and I don't have those."

The guide sheet seemed simple enough: current data on the witness, including name, date of birth, present address and contact information; place of residence during the war; and family status during the war. So far, I had everything I needed to create a preliminary application for Marian's editing.

The data on the rescuer was just as direct: full name, dates of birth and death, approximate age at the time. I knew all that as well. I continued to read the list of details required of someone naming a rescuer, and was stumped by the need for the present address of the rescuer's relatives and their telephone numbers. I had no idea if Stasio had living relatives or where I might find them. My initial Internet search had yielded people named Drabik living in Poland and in the United States, but I had no evidence suggesting any familial relationships. I suggested now that Marian submit the application and wait for researchers at Yad Vashem to help us find Stasio's relatives, assuming that they were indeed necessary for the honor to be bestowed.

Marian came for a subsequent visit and we sat at the kitchen table, as I read to him my initial draft of his story of Stasio. He suggested some changes and I sent him a final written testimony to include in the application:

The Department of the Righteous, Yad Vashem, Jerusalem, Israel

To Whom It May Concern:

My name is Marian Rosenbloom. I was born Marian Rozenblum, on March 7, 1930. I currently live at . . . New York, USA. . . . My telephone number is . . . and my e-mail address: . . . I have been retired for several years.

During the war, I lived in the Warsaw Ghetto and, for a period of time, in Praga. I was 9 years old when the Germans invaded Warsaw.

My rescuer's name was Stanislaw Drabik. According to a document retrieved from JewishGen.org, which I have attached to this testimony, he was born on February 1, 1902, in Warsaw, and died in Mauthausen-Gusen Concentration Camp on March 12, 1945. Stanislaw was single the last time I saw him in 1943. I do not know of any living relatives of Stanislaw Drabik.

I entered the Warsaw Ghetto in 1940, with my mother Rivka Rozenblum, my two older brothers, Leon and Hil Rozenblum, my twin brother Menache Rozenblum, and my older sister Elzbieta Rutman. My father Israel and my older brother Adam had escaped Poland and were somewhere in Russia during the war.

During the Ghetto Aktions of 1942, my mother and twin brother were both selected and sent to Treblinka. Leon and Hil were laborers in a German munitions factory in August of 1942. They were deported to Treblinka in the spring of 1943.

My sister Elzbieta and I survived the Aktions, along with her friends, the surviving members of the Rozenfarb family: Joseph, Danka, and Jacob.

When the Aktions continued and we realized that we too would be deported, Elzbieta was able to get in touch with Stanislaw Drabik, a Polish landowner who lived in Warsaw. She asked him for his help if we were to leave the Ghetto. He was the only person we could think of who might help us; we trusted him. Before the war, my father Israel had borrowed money from Stanislaw and they became friends.

One day, in January 1943, after a planned exit from the Ghetto, I showed up at Stanislaw's apartment. Stanislaw had gotten word to us that I could stay with him once I left the Ghetto. He greeted me, got me a plate to eat, and showed me what to do — where to stay and how to feed his dog. In the back of his apartment building, he had a farm where he was growing onions. I was there maybe for a month or two and then one of his tenants got suspicious and asked him, "What is that little boy doing here?" Stanislaw suspected that she would turn him in. He arranged for me to stay with a family who knew I was a Jew. They were paid for their help. Fearing for my safety when their neighbor seemed suspicious about me and my relationship to the family, Stanislaw had me return to his apartment to stay with him.

Since he was the property owner, he helped all of us: my sister Elzbieta; her friends, including the Rozenfarbs; and me. As a property owner, he was able to issue documents that gave proof of our residence at his address. He had a friend, a local priest, who gave us baptismal certificates with Polish names. I was Marian Rudski, Elzbieta was Elzbieta Rejewska.

When Elzbieta asked for help for some more of her friends, Stanislaw was again willing to help. Elzbieta had very close friends, the Goldmans. He was a banker before the war and she, Nora Goldman, was a professor of languages. Elzbieta got them out of the Ghetto and Stanislaw Drabik gave them identification papers and a safe place to stay on the Aryan side. Nora spoke perfect German and English and didn't look Jewish. She was very well educated and she couldn't sit still at the safe home Stanislaw had found for her; she had to find a job. She was able to find work as a translator outside of the city, but her German employer eventually found out that she was Jewish and she was arrested. Because she had identification papers that stated she lived at Stanislaw Drabik's address, they came to arrest him. At that time, I happened to be staying with Stanislaw a day or two each week. I wasn't supposed to be there very long, but I loved staying with him and his dog. I was there for a temporary stay when they arrested both of us.

The Gestapo arrived and knocked on his door before he realized they were there. They dealt with him in the front of the apartment and I was in the back, in the bedroom. The bedroom door was locked.

They asked him who was in the apartment with him and he told them that a friend's son was staying with him. They asked him to get me, so Stanislaw knocked at the bedroom door and said, "Marian, open the door." I opened the door and saw two men standing next to Stasio. They said, "Who are you?" I was half-dressed, half-asleep, and afraid to speak. Stanislaw repeated that I was "a friend." In Polish, the men told me to get dressed. The two men spoke Polish, but they were Gestapo.

The two men arrested Stanislaw and me, escorting us out of the house. I let the adults walk in front of me, hesitating just long enough to take in my options. There was a third man waiting for us in a car parked in front of the building. I circled around the back of the car to seemingly enter on the other side and sit next to Stanislaw. It was the fortuitous passing of a streetcar, just a few feet from the Gestapo's parked car, which brought me freedom and saved my life.

I was able to jump onto the streetcar and secure the distance and time I needed to find safety, before the Gestapo realized what had transpired. My trip lasted only one stop. Two Polish women witnessed my sudden arrival onto the moving car. Necessarily very vigilant, I watched them out of the corner of my eye as they leaned toward each other and mouthed the word "Jew." I jumped out onto the street before the conductor discovered my lack of funds and the women's assessment. I ran through the streets of Warsaw looking for a safe refuge. I never saw Stanislaw again. Nobody did.

The Sunday before our arrest, Stanislaw had taken me to visit his cousins. They had a building, a small building, on the other side of the river, in Praga. Stanislaw took me there, but didn't tell me a word about his family. His cousin had a wife and a child — they were a Polish family. That is where I ran when Stanislaw was arrested. His family took me in and showed me where I could hide. In the attic, they already had Elzbieta's friends, Joseph, Jacob, and Danka Rozenfarb, hiding behind a double wall.

They had a goat in the attic. Feeding the goat was their excuse for bringing food up to the attic. I don't remember their name. I wish I could. I was there for a year and a half. They were very nice people and we paid them for their help. Stanislaw was not paid for his.

I never saw Stanislaw again, not after the Gestapo took him away. He had been one of Elzbieta's connections to humanity, a remarkable rescuer.

Elzbieta, Jacob, Joseph, and Danka have all passed on. I am the only survivor rescued by Stanislaw that I know to be alive. It has taken me most of my life to have the courage to tell the story and do something — to name Stanislaw Drabik as my rescuer.

                             – Signed, Marian Rosenbloom, May 3, 2011

Marian received an e-mailed reply in a few weeks from Yad Vashem staff, beginning a lengthy but futile e-mail exchange.

"I received an e-mail from Yad Vashem on June 5th, asking for more information," Marian told me. "They wanted to know where Stanislaw lived during the war and where in Praga his cousins lived. They wanted addresses. I sent you a copy of the e-mail I sent back - "

> Dear Ms Rotman,
>
>   In reply to your e-mail regarding Stanislaw Drabik, he did reside during the war in Warsaw. To the best of my recollection the name of the street was Walska. Unfortunately, I do not remember the number.
>
>   I stayed in his place after leaving the Ghetto sometime in January of 1943. As to the address of his relative, I have no memory whatsoever, but it was in Praga, Warsaw.
>
>   I stayed in this place for about a year and half, until the Polish Uprising in August 1944.
>
>   I hope this information is helpful in considering the application.
>
>   *– Yours Truly, Marian Rosenbloom, June 8, 2011*

Marian received a response on June 9th. Ms Rotman, his contact person from Yad Vashem, noted that she was born and lived in Warsaw for thirty years and she only knew of a street named Wolska and not Walska. She acknowledged that it was a small mistake. She wanted the name of the street in Praga where Stasio's cousins lived, as well as their names. She ended her e-mail with a question: "Is there any chance you will get the information we need?"

Marian called me and expressed his frustration: "The person contacting me from Yad Vashem does not seem to have the resources we hoped would exist. I don't know if anything will come of this, but I will keep trying." So, he did:

> Dear Ms Rotman,
>
> Thank you very much for correcting the mistyped street Wolska. Regarding the street address on Praga–Warsaw and the names of Stanislaw's cousin I do not remember. The people that Stanislaw helped rescue and who could help me in providing you with that information have all passed away. I sincerely hope that this lack of information will not be an obstacle in honoring this man who gave his life to save the lives of others.
>
> *– Yours Truly, Marian Rosenbloom, June 10, 2011*

"I don't know if they will be able to help me find any relatives and if this is critical for my application," Marian told me as the summer approached. He was clearly eager for the application to succeed. Eager to honor his life-saving Stasio.

One day later that summer, arriving with a few moments to spare before a ceremony for Marian's grandson Michael, Bobby and I entered an unfamiliar synagogue along with our children and a curiously excited Ella. We had all travelled north to the upstate synagogue to witness a joyful milestone in our family. Marc's son Michael — Marian's only grandchild — was about to become a Bar Mitzvah.

I made my way through the crowd of happy tweens, teens, and adults, all eager to participate in the morning service and the reception to follow. I was looking for Marian when instead he found me; his face was wrinkled from the huge grin he could not contain. "I have something for you," he exclaimed, touching the breast pocket of his finely tailored suit.

I laughed during our embrace, retorting with my own revelation of a surprise for him as well. Hoping for a moment of quiet conversation, I had brought along a folder of old Polish newspapers. In the weeks before the anticipated family gathering, in my annual attempt to deal with the clutter in my basement, I had found yet another faded folder of Joseph's belongings. I must have overlooked this bulging collection of newspapers in my earlier search for Joseph's documents.

The yellowed newspapers, flaky and brittle to the touch, were dated from 1939 to 1945 and written in Polish. I could make out references to Hitler, the war, and Warsaw, but I could not determine where the newspapers had been printed or disseminated. I needed Marian's help to make sense of the newspapers and why Bobby's father Joseph had saved them.

Marian had his own pressing need to talk and share: "Look at what I found," he said, excitedly reaching into his jacket pocket and handing me a yellow-tinted plastic folder containing a brown cardboard packet. "I knew I had it somewhere and I found it. It's for you," he added with a tender smile.

I tried to slide the worn and stained yellow ochre casing from its plastic holder, not realizing that I had been rendered multi-thumbed by the German words printed on the cover. The German text surrounded a photograph of Marian, when he himself was not yet thirteen. "*Meldekarte für Juden*" was printed at the top of the jacket cover, above the words *"Der Jude"* followed by *"Rozenblum Moisze Icchok"* typed on the dotted line. The swastika stamp overlapping Marian's face gave me a chill.

"It's my working papers," Marian blurted out, impatient with my inability to comprehend what I was holding.

"Look at the signatures next to Toebbens's stamp. It is dated August 10, 1942, and Bauch's stamp is dated the 31st of December, 1942, and again for February 28th, 1943."

I tried to make sense of the dates of the stamps, knowing that Marian had left the Ghetto in January of 1943. They had to have signified the termination of the work status. Marian had carried the folder with him when he left the Ghetto; he never gave it up. I found two smaller folders inside, all stamped and dated for Moisze Icchok Rozenblum, born March 7, 1929, in Warsaw, and living at 34 Leszno, Warsaw. Marian, born in 1930, had lied about the year of his birth in order to get working papers.

"I have kept them all these years. Now they are yours for safekeeping," Marian said, grasping my hands in his.

It was our own ceremony of sorts. I looked into Marian's gray-blue eyes and smiled back, knowing that I had taken a huge burden from his shoulders, and that it was my task to make sense, and somehow art, from his pain.

The Bar Mitzvah ceremony began and Marian's grandson Michael, leading the services like a mensch, stood at the dais, flanked by Marian, Bobby, and our son Seth. It was a moving rite of passage.

When the rabbi asked Marian to pass the Torah to Marc, who then passed it to Michael, he described how this same ritual had occurred when Marian's grandfather had passed his Torah to Marian's father and then to Marian. It was the tradition of generations of Jewish men, overseeing the Bar Mitzvah of their sons and grandsons. I looked at Marian, in this moment of reflection, and felt my own throat tighten along with his. I could not hold back the rush of tears that flowed from Marian's eyes, down my cheeks.

Lisa passed me tissues as I sobbed quietly in my seat. Contrary to the rabbi's remarks, and in a heartfelt break in Jewish tradition, Marian had not been a Bar Mitzvah. He was hiding from the Nazis when he turned thirteen — there was no family or community of Jews to make the ceremony, to celebrate his achievements, to witness his reading of the Torah. The one person in our family who could recite passages in Hebrew with his eyes closed, Marian had never felt the need to have a Bar Mitzvah. Surviving had been enough. Somehow this day honoring Michael seemed a day of healing for Marian.

After the ceremony, Marian and I sat together munching on appetizers as he looked through the newspapers. He recognized the print used by the Germans; Joseph's newspaper collection had been printed and distributed in Warsaw, but in the German-occupied part of the city. Joseph had chosen to save the papers for some reason other than their value as vestiges of the Ghetto. Marian could find nothing of significance in the articles. I placed the fragile papers in a plastic bag, hoping to salvage the age-burned sheets for display in a Holocaust museum.

"Have you heard anything more from Yad Vashem?" I asked.

"No, nothing else."

Early in November of 2012, nearly six months after prior correspondence about Stasio Drabik and Yad Vashem, Marian received a letter requesting the name and contact information for any other living relative of his who might have had any additional information or who could corroborate Marian's story. Marian wrote back:

> Dear Ms Rotman,
>
> I am pleased to advise you that my sister Elzbieta had one son whose name and address are as follows: Dr. Robert Rostan . . . Woodbury, N.Y. He is aware of the case regarding

Drabik and he will be happy to cooperate with you. You may be interested to know that Danka Rozenfarb had two daughters who are currently residing in Canada. Stanislaw had provided housing for the family of Rozenfarbs. I don't know whether their mother had told them about the work Stanislaw Drabik did on behalf of many Jews, not just the Rozenfarbs and the Rozenblums.

With regard to the number of Wolska Street where Drabik lived, I have no recollection. It was a two-family house; he occupied the first floor, the second floor was rented. Behind the house was a large plot of land where he grew onions. He was the owner of the place. I was with him in the house when he was arrested. Thank you very much for your cooperation.

– *Marian Rosenbloom, November 5, 2012*

Bobby expected to hear promptly from Yad Vashem's researcher. He did not.

"Have you heard from Yad Vashem?" I asked Marian later that month during his visit on Thanksgiving Day.

"No, not yet, but when we finish with Stasio, we will apply for the Kudelskis," he replied, with optimism and a smile. "Kudelski provided safe housing for the entire family near the end of the war as well as after. Surely Yad Vashem will recognize him! Elsa kept in touch with him and his family and sent gifts every year, for as long as she was able. Did you know that?"

"Yes," I replied, understanding now, as much as I ever could, the importance of the gesture that Elzbieta had made an essential part of her life.

Marian's story was shared at last, and the prospect of honoring the Kudelskis — even though Stasio's honoring would likely not happen — brightened our thoughts. . . .

· · ·

A stunning surprise still awaited us. On the eve of Passover in March 2013, nearly two years after the last correspondence with Ms Rotman at Yad Vashem, I called Marian to wish him a happy holiday. He was having a Seder — commemorating the exodus of the Hebrews from captivity in Egypt — with his family in upstate New York while we had our downstate Seder with our children and my mother Joan. My mother had flown in from Florida the Friday night before the holiday and we busied ourselves cooking the traditional brisket and chicken soup and baking a sponge cake. Marian came to the phone with obvious excitement in his voice.

"I found Stanislaw!" he exclaimed.

"How? What do you mean?" I responded.

"I googled 'Drabich Stanislaw Warsaw Poland'! Can you imagine? I just sent you an e-mail with the information. He was sent to the Pawiak Prison after his arrest. The Stanislaw Drabik we found and thought was Stasio, the one sent to Mauthausen-Gusen, was not him. The spelling is different too. I couldn't have known that," Marian explained.

"Stasio had a brother Józef, an attorney, who died in 1972. I knew he had a brother — a lawyer — Stasio told me about him — but I could not remember his name. Perhaps we should contact Yad Vashem again!"

I was speechless, trying to plan our next move and take in the scope of the new information. Apparently, after reading what we thought was the final version of his story, Marian had tried once again to somehow find Stasio's living relatives, or at least some evidence that Stasio had existed. He did what I had done so many times in the past without any luck: he googled both "Stanislaw Drabik" and "Stanislaw Drabich." This time he found an entry on a public posting of a family tree. The posting had been there for one year.

"Let me take a look at the information and I'll get back to you before we do anything," I cautioned. I did exactly what Marian had described doing himself and found the following in a family tree posted from Warsaw by Aleksander Kopiński: "Stanislaw Franciszek Drabich; Birthdate: April 15, 1907; Birthplace: Warsaw, Masovian Voivodeship, Poland; Death: July 16, 1943; Cause of Death: Died at Warsaw's Pawiak Prison."

I wondered why Marian hadn't called instead of e-mailing me with such extraordinary news. I soon learned why—

"Marian, I followed through with your lead and I've contacted the manager of the family tree," I told him minutes after our last phone conversation.

"I know it's the same Stanislaw!" Marian exclaimed. "They sent him to Pawiak Prison. That's what the family entered next to his name. I knew that prison. It was near the apartment Elsa and I shared in the Ghetto. They tortured prisoners there. After May 1943 when the Ghetto had been turned into ruins, executions were carried out in the streets near the prison. It must have been an awful death for him. My God, he never told about the others in hiding. They must have tortured him while the family hid in Praga and he never told them about us," Marian added, in a more solemn note to his discovery.

I understood, at that moment, why he had not shouted the news from his rooftop. He had always believed Stasio was killed after the arrest, but the images he himself had of the Pawiak Prison made the fact excruciatingly hard to suffer.

"Let's not contact Yad Vashem until we're sure it is Stasio's family," I said, trying to be calm, objective — careful in my processing and handling of the bittersweet news.

"I will wait for you to hear from them," he said, trying, unsuccessfully, to control his excitement.

He didn't have to wait very long. Within a few hours, I was in dialogue with Aleksander Kopiński, Stasio's distant relative, who lived in Warsaw.

Aleksander,

I am trying to locate the family of a Stanislaw Drabich who lived in Warsaw in the 1940s on Wolska Street. I believe he owned the building he lived in and grew onions in his yard. He was a good friend of my husband's grandfather and my husband's uncle, who was present when Stanislaw was arrested by the Germans. I do know that his brother was an attorney. Any help from you would be greatly appreciated.

> – *Sincerely, Susan Rostan*
> *Sunday, March 24, 2013, 1:35 pm*

Susan,

I guess that you've just found them. Congratulations. Stanislaw, whose profile you've mentioned, lived on 107, and then 105 Wolska Str. with his parents and brother Józef, who was a lawyer. Unfortunately, Stanislaw was murdered by German Nazis while participating in the Warsaw uprising during World War 2 in 1944, as well as some tens of thousands in that area (Wola) inhabitants, among them many relatives and neighbours. But his brother's descendants still live in Warsaw.

> – *Regards, a.k. [Aleksander Kopiński], 7:53 pm*

I was astounded at the timing of this new correspondence, and glad at Aleksander's proficiency in English. I was confused about the "participation in the Warsaw Uprising," but held on to the belief that this was "our" Stasio. And so I responded:

Aleksander,

Thank you for getting back to me. You have made my uncle very happy. Stanislaw Drabich saved his life, my mother-in-law's life, as well as my husband's father and family and countless other friends. For this, and more, he is to be remembered.

— Susan Rostan, 8:44 pm

Susan,

I'm glad that my information was helpful. Perhaps you could write a bit about your family's history concerning Drabichs. I would tell it to Stanislaw's brother's grandchildren, who might not know it. On the other hand, forgive my mistake: Stanisław was killed by Gestapo about a year before Warsaw uprising, in Pawiak prison. But many people there in Wolska 105 and 107 were murdered in 1944, including over 10 persons from houseowner's family Grabowski, who were our relatives too.

— a.k., 9:01 pm

Aleksander,

I will do much more. I have written a book about my husband's family and how Stanislaw saved them. You are correct about Stanislaw being arrested by the Gestapo in 1943. My uncle was there, with him. Do you know who the relatives in Praga were? They also helped my husband's family.

— Susan Rostan, 9:11 pm

Susan,

That's great! Could you tell me if he was involved in the organization Zegota that was saving Jews?

— a.k., Monday, March 25, 4:04 am

I knew about Zegota from my research. It was a code name for the "Polish Council to Aid Jews," an underground organization of Polish resistance in German-occupied Poland. Operating under the auspices of the Polish Government in Exile, from 1942 to 1945, Zegota's specific purpose was to aid the country's Jews and find places of safety for them in Poland. Poland was the only country in occupied Europe where this kind of secret organization existed. And so I responded to Aleksander:

Aleksander,

I do not know if Stanislaw was a member of Zegota. I do know that he was a business associate and friend of my husband's grandfather Israel Rozenblum. It is because of this connection that he saved our family. Some members were hidden in Stanislaw's cousins' home in Praga, in their attic, for over a year. I would like to find their names. Our uncle, Marian Rosenbloom, has nominated Stanislaw for recognition by Yad Vashem, as one of the Righteous Among the Nations, but they were not able to find any surviving relatives. I too have been searching since 2009. Marian found your posting on Google yesterday and now we have the answers. I really would love to have a picture of Stanislaw. That would mean so much to our family, none of whom would be here today without his help.

    – *Susan, 8:08 am*

Susan,

Thanks a lot for your answer. I'm very pleased that my family history work helped us to get in contact. It's necessary to make everything we can to remember Stanislaw, as he's been never mentioned as candidate for the title of Righteous or even one of the Polish WW2 saviors of Jews so far. I don't understand one thing: why Yad Vashem has not managed to find living relatives of him or the people he saved. I know his brother Józef's daughter, and daughter-in-law, as well as his grandson and granddaughter. Do you think it's possible to resume this case in Jerusalem?

Obviously I'll tell the Drabichs about your request, and ask
if they have any photo of Stanislaw.

    – a.k., 8:27 am

So now I knew that Stasio's brother Józef had lived until 1972,
leaving children and grandchildren behind in Warsaw.

Aleksander,

    Marian is contacting Yad Vashem this morning. He is
very eager to continue the process of having Stanislaw recognized, as we have been working on this for several years.
Do you have a direct contact address for yourself or Józef's
family so that Marian can pass this on to Yad Vashem ?

    – Susan, 8:57 am

In the meantime, Marian had composed a letter to Yad Vashem,
informing them of his discovery:

Dear Ms Rotman,

    I wish to advise you that I have found the address of
Stanislaw Drabich by searching Google: "Drabich Stanislaw
Warsaw Poland."

    This is what I have found: Stanislaw Franciszek Drabich;
born April 15, 1907, in Warsaw, Masovian Voivodeship,
Poland; died 1943; cause of death: Zginal na Pawiaku.

    We have gotten in touch with Mr Aleksander Kopiński,
who gave Stasio's address as 105 then 107 Wolska Street.
Feel free to contact him.

    In the process of further study, I learned that there is a
telephone directory thanks to Yad Vashem. Could you
please look up his telephone number? I recall using his
phone while staying in his house.

I have asked Dr Robert Rostan, the son of my sister, if
Yad Vashem has contacted him. His answer was *no*. He
could shed some light as to the validity of my testimony.

I respectfully request that Yad Vashem resolve my request
to honor this man who gave his life to save many Jews.

Wishing you a Happy Passover.

– Yours, truly, Marian Rosenbloom, March 25, 5:24 am

Several hours later Marian received a reply: they would try to find
a telephone listing at 105 or 107 Wolska Street and they wanted
Bobby's e-mail and home addresses. Marian had not been clear about
the telephone directory. He was referring to the 1939/40 Warsaw directory that Yad Vashem had in their own archives. Marian had hoped for
more proof that Stasio had lived at 105 or 107 Wolska Street in 1943.

Once again, Marian sent Yad Vashem our e-mail and home
addresses. At the bottom of his e-mail, Marian added a request for Ms
Rotman: "Please give this matter your prompt attention since time is of
the essence."

Three days later Yad Vashem sent Bobby an e-mail with the following questions: "What do you know about the person who helped your
mother during the II world war. Is there any documentation your
mother wrote about her rescue?"

Bobby felt frustrated and angry. Almost two years had passed since
Marian sent his testimony and Yad Vashem was first making contact
with him. He answered the questions after carefully composing his
response. Marian's words had added a sense of urgency to this quest
and he wanted to be succinct, without repeating exactly what Marian
had already submitted to Yad Vashem, which was all we knew:

Dear Ms Rotman,

My mother Elizabeth Lowenthal and my Uncle Marian
Rosenbloom never spoke of their experiences during the

war. It has only been very recently, in the past few years, that Marian has begun to share the story of their lives in Warsaw. This has been very difficult for Marian, to this I can testify.

I have learned of Stasio's altruism through Marian's revelations and there is no reason on earth for me to doubt the veracity of his story. I wish I could tell you that I have written proof or that my mother corroborated Marian's testimony, but I cannot. She would not talk about her experiences, even when I dared to ask.

Marian is the living documentation you need to honor Stasio Drabich for sheltering and caring for Marian and securing the necessary papers and safe homes for my mother and father and my father's family. We have just learned that Stasio was incarcerated at Pawiak before he died and not at Mauthausen-Gusen as we had previously believed. Marian remembers what happened to people sent to Pawiak and there is no doubt that Stasio never revealed the location of the safe houses he secured for my family. He was a man of integrity and valor. Without his life-saving help I would not be here, nor would my own family.

Marian's precious memories of the particulars of Stasio's help and the time they spent together are all we have to offer you, and I swear by them.

– Robert J. Rostan, March 28, 2013

While we waited for a response, Marian called to tell me he had forwarded two photographs of Stasio sent to him by Józef's granddaughter Aleksandra. I opened the first attachment and found a young mustachioed Stasio in a formal portrait. His mustache curved above his upper lip like the wings of a bird. The second photograph, taken at a later date, depicted Stasio in a long overcoat and fedora, gloves in hand as he walked down a Warsaw street. This was the Stasio that Marian remembered. Aleksandra had written Marian an e-mail thanking him:

Marian –

If there is anything else we could do, please do not hesitate to contact us. I wish to thank you from all my heart that you kept the memory of Stanislaw and that you shared your experience with us. That in a sense returned to us the member of our family of who, till that moment, we only knew that he existed and died during World War II like so many others. . . . Could you write us more about your later fortune? How did you manage to survive? Did anyone else from your family survive?

– Best Regards, Aleksandra,
Thursday, March 28, 2013, 4:35 pm

Her words came at me like a lifting wave within the tumultuous flood of emotions that Marian and I had been experiencing. Astounded by the discovery of Stasio's family — his living relatives and Stasio's last known address — we felt we were close to the ending we so desperately wanted. Satisfying the Yad Vashem requests at last would have sufficed. Aleksandra's letter gave us so much more.

Aleksandra had made us aware of still another story — the story of a son lost, with no explanation. Stasio had disappeared from the Drabich family and all they knew was that he had been taken to a Warsaw prison — a prison famous for its torture and public executions. Marian had given Stasio's family what they needed, what they so deeply deserved: an explanation — a story of Stasio's noble life. Truly, this was much more than Marian or I ever thought we would or could do, once I began . . . digging.

In July of 2013 Stanislaw Drabich was officially recognized as one of the Righteous Among the Nations.

Family Photographs for Ella

Young Marian Rozenblum, summer 1939.

Elzbieta—at first glimpse a teen in the 1930s, yet more likely from a Nazi work card portrait after 1939. . . . At far left, Elzbieta's mother Rivka Wilde Rozenblum (standing, l) as a teen, her mother (standing r) and her two sisters, early 1900s.

Below, Four among friends—Israel Rozenblum (3rd from l) with Elzbieta, her husband Benjamin (light coat), her brother Adam, mid-1930s.

At left, Elzbieta's brother Leon (l) with parents Rivka and Israel at a family wedding for Adam or Elzbieta.

Above, Rivka with (from l) sons Menache, Marian, and Hil, late summer 1939. . . . At left, Marian and the lighter-weight Menache playing acrobats, late summer 1939.

The Album of Pictures, *compiled by Elzbieta and others to document the war experience. . . . Below, memorial gravestone in Paris for Rozenblum family members killed by the Nazis: Rivka, Leon, Hil, Menache.*

Above, Marian's work card at age 12, for Toebbens's workshop, Warsaw Ghetto . . . . Stanislaw Drabich—later the rescuer of Marian, Elzbieta, the Rozenfarbs, and so many others—in pre-war Warsaw.

After the war, above, Elzbieta reunited with Yael in Tel Aviv, 1960 . . . and earlier seated with Yael and Joseph, Paris 1948, with family and friends. Elzbieta's father Israel stands at left, behind his French wife.

Marian, Elzbieta, and baby Robert with his grandfather Israel, Paris 1950.

Elzbieta with Bobby en route to the United States in 1956, aboard the Liberté, Manhattan skyline in the distance . . . and relaxing in her hammock in Long Island.

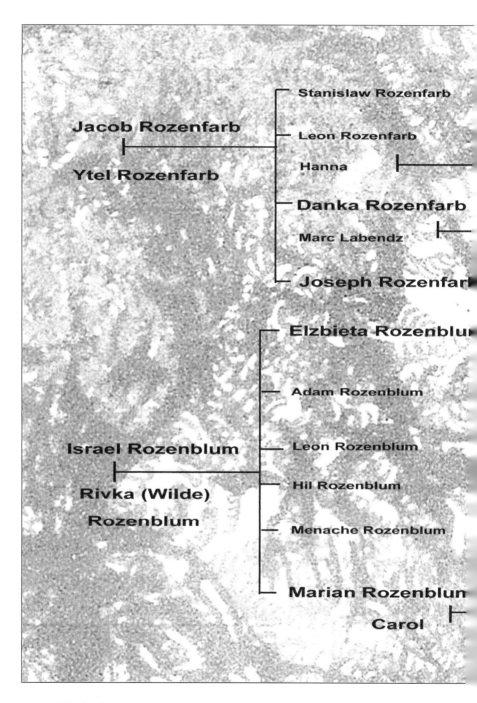

Jacob Rozenfarb

Ytel Rozenfarb

Stanislaw Rozenfarb

Leon Rozenfarb

Hanna

Danka Rozenfarb

Marc Labendz

Joseph Rozenfarb

Elzbieta Rozenblum

Adam Rozenblum

Israel Rozenblum

Rivka (Wilde)
Rozenblum

Leon Rozenblum

Hil Rozenblum

Menache Rozenblum

Marian Rozenblum

Carol

Branches from Ella's Family Tree

:dzislaw Rozenfarb

— Eliane Labendz

— Robert Rostan

Susan Rostan

- Seth Rostan
- Lianne Rostan
- Adam Rostan
- Lisa — Ella

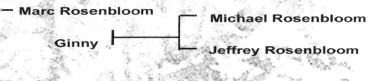

— Marc Rosenbloom

Ginny

— Ira Rosenbloom

- Michael Rosenbloom
- Jeffrey Rosenbloom

Selected Resources

The following books and Internet sites were crucial to the writing of *Digging*:

Notes from the Warsaw Ghetto, from the Journal of Emmanuel Ringelblum, translated and edited by Jacob Sloan (ibooks, inc., 2006), was most useful for background, as were *Words to Outlive Us: Eyewitness Accounts from the Warsaw Ghetto,* edited by Michal Grynberg and translated by Philip Boehm (Picador, 2002); *Witness: Voices from the Holocaust,* edited by Joshua M. Greene and Shiva Kumar (Simon & Schuster, 2000); *Poland Under Nazi Occupation,* by Janusz Gumkowski and Kazimierz Leszczynski (Polonia Publishing House, 1961); *Survivors of the Holocaust in Poland: A Portrait Based on Jewish Community Records 1944-47,* by Lucjan Dobroszycki (M. E. Sharpe, Inc., 1994); and *I remember,* by Dov Visberg (Freund Publishing House Limited, 1998); Ancestry.com; The Jewish Historical Institute: www.jhi.pl; YIVO Encyclopedia of Jews in Eastern Europe: www.yivoencyclopedia.org; Jewish Records Indexing Poland and the Jewish Historical Institute Warsaw, in cooperation with the Jewish Genealogical Society, NY: www.jewishgen.org/jri-pl/jri-jhi.htm. SMR

About the Author

Susan M. Rostan is a visual artist and has an MFA from Long Island University, and a doctorate in gifted education from Columbia University. Ms Rostan has directed the Rostan Art School since 1970 and has served as an adjunct professor in Hofstra University's School of Education. She has conducted extensive research in children's artistic development, publishing well-received articles in *The Journal of Creative Behavior* and *Creativity Research Journal* as well as chapters in diverse books on creativity.

Ms Rostan and her husband Robert live on Long Island.